INTRODUCTION OF MR. MARKET

PREM AMRIT

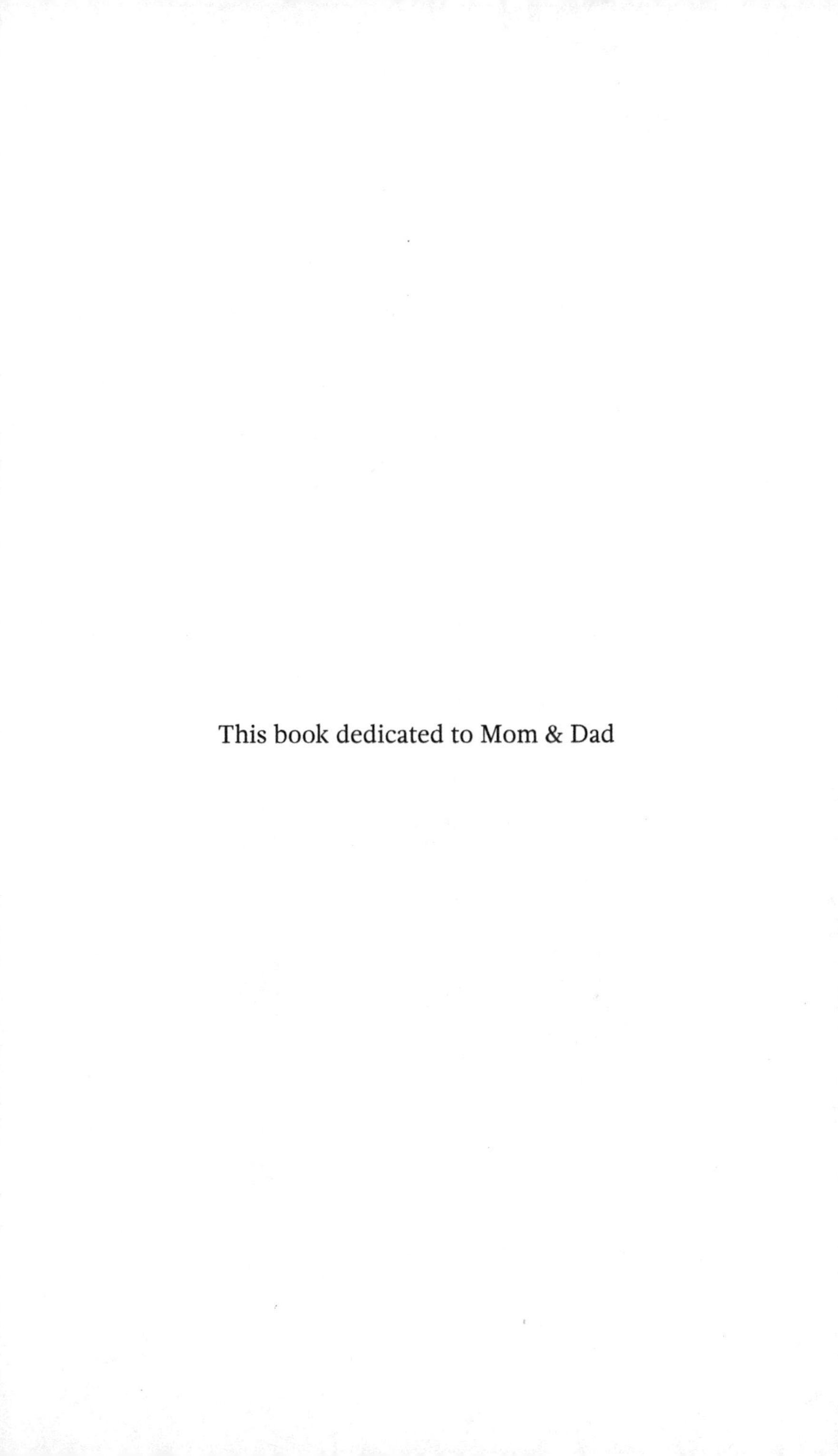

This book dedicated to Mom & Dad

Contents

Foreword

In this book, you read about the share market. This book is for every new person who wants to start an investment journey in the share market. This is my Second book and I try to give valuable content.

Share market is where buying and selling of shares happens. A share represents a unit of ownership of the company from where you bought it. It is a place where shares of public listed companies are traded. The stock market consists of exchanges in which stock shares and other financial securities of publicly held companies are bought and sold.

CHAPTER ONE

STOCK MARKET

Do you feel confused when you hear about the stock market? Is this an area you really want to study but can't seem to master? To be sure, you are not alone in feeling this way.

Could a lack of confidence in how the stock market works also make you quit investing? It doesn't have to be this way. We can help you understand what the stock market is and how it works, making investing less overwhelming.

What is a stock?

Stocks are an investment. When you buy stock in a company, you also buy a small portion of that company, which we call "shares."

Stock is a certificate issued by a joint-stock company to shareholders as a certificate for investing in shares and a certificate for claiming dividends. Like ordinary commodities, stocks have prices, can be bought and sold, and can be used as collateral. A joint-stock company raises money by issuing shares.

The word "share" in English is share, and the definition of share itself is the meaning of sharing and sharing. If we put it in vernacular terms, you can think of holding "shares" as "sharing" ownership of a company with others.

Investors can buy stocks of companies they think will grow better and better. If the company grows better, the company's stock will appreciate. After the stock appreciates, investors can sell the stock at a profit.

Definition of a stock:

Stocks are securities of ownership in a company.

The English of securities is securities, which is derived from the word secure. Secure means safety and security, and is designed to make investors who buy part of the company's ownership shares feel safe and secure when they get the paper "securities". The Chinese word "securities" can be thought of as a voucher that proves, a document that proves that you have ownership of a company.

For companies, issuing stock is a way to raise capital and expand the company's business. **For investors,** stocks are a way to allow their money to grow and overcome inflation over time.

When you own stock in a company, you are a shareholder and you get a share of the profits the company generates.

Companies can sell their shares directly without going through a stock market exchange, deciding how many shares to issue, and the price of the shares. Investors can also buy these shares directly from the company without going through a brokerage.

Companies can also choose to go public. Listing a company requires selling shares through a stock market exchange, such as the Nasdaq, the New York Stock Exchange, **NSE** India (**National Stock Exchange** of India Ltd), or **Bombay Stock Exchange (BSE)**.

Investors can trade these stocks with each other through brokerages, and this behaviour forms the stock market. In the stock market, the supply and demand of stocks directly affects the price of stocks.

500 years ago, a Venetian lender was buying and selling debt with other lenders. These lenders fill the void of large banks and provide easier loan options for the general public due to the relatively high threshold for large banks to lend.

These lenders would buy and sell loans to each other. We all know that not all lenders can afford to pay their debts, so it is beneficial for lenders to be able to sell some high-risk, high-interest loans from time to time, and some people will buy these loans for investment purposes. .

Slowly, this market naturally evolved into the fact that lenders also began to buy and sell government debt, forming a large market for buying and selling debt. This market hasn't started using the word "stock" yet, but it's the foundation of the stock market.

The world's first publicly traded company

The East India Company is recognized as the world's first publicly traded company.

In the 16th century, the Dutch, British and French governments granted royal franchises to companies named after the word "East India".

At the height of imperialism, every Westerner seemed to benefit from the East Indies and Asia. However, sailing at sea is very dangerous, not only with the Barbary pirates, but also in poor weather and sailing conditions.

In order to reduce the losses caused by sailing risks, ship owners have been looking for investors for a long time, and the investors will provide equipment for the ship and crew at their expense. If the voyage is successful, they receive a percentage of the proceeds in return. In the early days, these LLCs usually only made one voyage. When it's over, it's dissolved and a new company is formed for the next voyage.

When the "East India" companies were formed, they decided to change the way they did business. These companies instead issue shares, which pay dividends, which are paid out of the entire proceeds of all voyages, rather than on a per voyage basis.

This allowed the "East India" companies to claim more shares and build a larger fleet. The size of the company, combined with the fact that the Royal Franchise leaves them with no competition, means shareholders can make huge profits.

Would you like some coffee, and stock?

Since the shares of East Indian companies were issued on paper, investors could sell their shares to other investors.

There were no stock exchanges at the time, so investors had to find brokers to trade. In the UK, most brokers and investors trade in coffee shops near London.

Bond offerings and shares for sale are handwritten, posted on store doors, or mailed out.

Stock prices fluctuate on a daily basis, but as an investor, you will want the stock you buy to increase in value over time.

However, not every company's stock value will rise. The company may not develop well, or go out of business entirely. When this happens, investors may lose some or all of their investment.

That's why stock investors need to learn to diversify and buy stocks in many different companies, rather than focusing on just one company.

Stocks have the following characteristics:

- **Responsibility:** As the certificate of property rights or equity, the stock is the securities performance of the stock, and represents the certain rights and responsibilities of the shareholders to the company issuing the stock. Shareholders participate in the company's operation and management by participating in the general meeting of shareholders and exercising voting rights; shareholders can receive dividends from the company and participate in dividends with the stocks they hold, and have the right to claim compensation for the company's assets under certain conditions; shareholders are limited to the shares they hold. Responsible. Shareholders' equity is proportional to their share of the company's share capital.

- **Liquidity:** As a kind of negotiable securities, stocks can be used as collateral and can be exchanged for cash through transfer and sale in the stock market at any time, thus becoming a highly liquid and liquid asset.

- **Risk:** In addition to receiving certain dividends, stock investors may also earn bid-ask spread profits in the stock market. However, the uncertainty of investment returns makes stock investment more risky. Generally speaking, the higher the expected return, the greater the risk. The poor operating conditions of the companies that issue stocks, or even bankruptcy, the large fluctuations in the stock market and investors' own decision-making mistakes may bring different degrees of risk to investors.

- **Indefinite:** Stock investment is a long-term investment with no fixed period. As long as the company exists, investors generally cannot withdraw shares in the middle.

- **Statutory:** Stocks must be approved and registered by the relevant institutions, and can only be issued after obtaining a visa, and must be in a legal form to record legal matters.

CHAPTER TWO

HOW DO STOCKS WORK?

Companies often raise money by selling stock, and then use the money for various activities.

The role of stocks, shares and equity is to give you direct exposure to company performance. When the company's performance is good, the stock price will rise, and when the company's performance is bad, the stock price will fall.

Stock exchanges facilitate the exchange of shares of listed companies. There are several ways a company can go public, but the more traditional and most common is when a company conducts an initial public offering (IPO) .

For example, a company may use the funds raised by issuing shares to finance new products or production lines, expand operations or pay down debt.

Once a company's stock is listed, it can be bought and sold among investors.

An initial public offering of stock by a company is called an IPO. Once a company's stock is listed, it can be bought and sold among investors.

If you buy publicly traded stock, you usually don't buy it from the company itself, but from another investor who wants to sell the stock. Likewise, if you want to sell a stock, you are also selling to another investor who wants to buy.

This naturally formed market is called the stock market.

And how are these transactions carried out? These transactions are made through stock exchanges, where stockbrokers (brokers) trade on behalf of each investor.

Many investors now use stock brokerage companies (brokers) on the Internet to buy and sell stocks through the broker's trading platform.

Let's break it down in detail, starting with the basics. Stocks, also known as equity, are securities that represent fractional ownership of a public company. So, when you buy stock in a company, you own a piece of that company. Shares are units of stock; the more shares you buy, the more shares you own in a company. Companies issue stock to raise capital and grow their business.

There are two main types of stock, one called common stock and the other called preferred stock. The main difference between the two is that common stock gives shareholders the right to vote on the company's affairs and participate in the growth of the company's earnings, while preferred stock does not. Preferred stock may pay higher fixed dividends.

What is the stock market?

A simple way to think about the stock market is to think of it as a network of stock exchanges where traders and investors buy and sell shares of public companies.

Unlisted companies list their shares on exchanges through a process called an initial public offering (IPO). Investors buy these shares, enabling companies to raise money from the public to grow their businesses. Once a company is listed on a stock exchange, it is now a public company, and investors can buy and sell the company's shares on an exchange that tracks the share price.

Supply and demand help determine the price of each security that investors and traders are willing to buy and sell.

What are stocks, shares and equity?

Stock, shares and equity are terms used to describe the ownership unit of one or more companies. The owners, the shareholders, (if granted by the company) receive dividend payments as well as voting rights.

These terms are often used interchangeably, but in essence there are some potentially confusing differences between stocks, shares, and equity.

"Stock" is often used to refer to fractional ownership of multiple companies - for example, you could say you own stock in Amazon and Microsoft

"Share" usually refers to a unit of ownership in a particular company - for example, you could say you own 10 Amazon shares

"Equity" is a term that refers to total ownership of a company - for example, if a company owns 10,000 shares and you own 1,000 of them, you could say you own 10% of the company.

CHAPTER THREE

HOW DOES THE STOCK MARKET WORK?

To better understand how the stock market works, it is helpful to know that there are two types of markets, namely: **primary markets and secondary markets.**

primary markets and secondary markets

Primary market

The primary market is where securities are created and companies list their shares through an IPO. Remember, an IPO is when a company goes public for the first time.

secondary market

The secondary market is essentially a stock exchange, where these stocks (and the thousands of others on the market) are bought, sold and traded on a daily basis. The Indian Stock Exchange is open from 9:30 a.m. to 3:30 p.m. on Monday to Friday, and the New York Stock Exchange is open from 9:30 a.m. to 4:00 p.m. (ET) Monday through Friday, The Nasdaq follows the same opening and closing schedule as the NYSE.

There are two main types of investment strategies when trading stocks on the stock exchange.

Day trading, as the name suggests, is buying and selling the same stock throughout the day, sometimes lasting minutes or even seconds. The aim is to take advantage of small fluctuations in price.

Then, there are more long-term deals or investments, where buyers hold the stock for longer and look to capitalise on the company's long-term earnings growth.

The stock market serves two important purposes.

First, it helps companies raise money (often referred to as capital) from the public by issuing stock, which is used to finance the company and expand its business.

Second, it offers investors who buy these stocks an opportunity to share in the company's profits. Investors can profit from holding stocks in one of two ways. Some stocks pay regular dividends (a given amount per share), providing a return on the amount invested in the stock. Alternatively, capital appreciation can also be used to earn returns when the stock price rises.

Why should a company be listed on the stock market?

Companies are listed on the stock market and raise capital by selling their shares to institutional or retail investors. Institutional investors refer to entities such as investment funds or banks, while retail investors refer to ordinary people.

Most companies are listed on domestic exchanges. For example, in the UK, most stocks are listed on the London Stock Exchange (LSE) or the Alternative Investment Market (AIM). In India most stocks are listed on the BSE OR NSE.

Even so, it is becoming more common for companies to go public multiple times in order to take advantage of foreign direct investment.

How much stock can a company issue?

The minimum number of shares a company can issue is 1 share, in which case the entire company may have only one owner. However, there is no unified upper limit on how many shares a company can issue, depending on each company's own circumstances.

The number of shares in circulation can also change as companies can issue additional shares or buy back shares from investors.

How much is a stock worth?

Different stocks have different values. The value of a stock depends on whether you are looking at its fair value or market value, where fair value is the intrinsic value of a stock based on the company's fundamentals, and market value is the price at which an individual is currently willing to buy the underlying stock.

The fair value of a stock tends to be much lower than the market value because the latter is susceptible to demand, which does not always reflect the fundamentals of the stock. If the demand for a stock rises and the supply stays the same, the stock price will rise because people are willing to pay more for it.

CHAPTER FOUR

WHY TRADE STOCKS?

People trade stocks to take advantage of profit opportunities arising from developments in the global economy and the growth prospects of individual companies.

How to trade stocks? Or How are stocks traded?

Not everyone who buys and sells stocks is a so-called "stock trader."

Most investors are divided into two types, one is a "trader" (like the protagonist of the movie Wolf of Wall Street), and the other is an "investor" (like Warren Buffet).

The difference between "**trader**" and "**investor**" is that the term "**stock trader**" usually refers to the regular buying and selling of stocks, taking advantage of daily price fluctuations to profit.

The goal of this short-term trade is to see how much money you can make in the next minute, hour, day, or month, unlike investing in stocks for the long term.

There are **Active Trading** and **Day trading / frequent trading** in stock trading.

Active Trading and Day trading

Active trading

Active trading refers to investors who conduct 10 or more transactions per month. Active trading strategies rely primarily on market timing, taking advantage of short-term events (company or market volatility) to profit in the weeks or months ahead.

Day Trading

Day Trading refers to an investor's strategy of buying, selling and liquidating a stock within one trading day (closing a position means no longer holding a stock or fund).

A day trader's goal is to see how much he can make in the next few minutes, hours or days, not too concerned about the company's operations.

To trade stocks, you need to follow these 6 steps to get started.

Open an account with a brokerage

You need to open a trading account with a broker to start trading stocks.

Set your trading budget

When setting your trading budget, remember not to use the funds you need for your usual expenses, as well as your emergency and retirement savings, and only invest what you can afford to lose.

I would also recommend that you don't allocate more than 10% of your funds to a single stock as volatility can be huge.

In general, you can allocate 10% to your retirement savings, 10% to your emergency fund, and invest the rest you won't need in addition to your usual expenses.

Learn to use Market Order and Limit Order

Once you've opened a trading account and set a budget, you can start trading stocks using the broker's trading platform.

You will see several different buy and sell order types, which will determine how your trade will be executed.

The 2 most common order types are:

Market Order:

Market Order: Buy or sell stocks at the best price at the moment.

Limit Order:

Limit Order: Buy or sell a stock at a specific price. In the case of a "buy" order, the limit price is the highest bid price you are willing to pay, and the order will only go through if the stock price falls below that price.

Open a practice account

Many brokerages offer demo trading accounts that allow you to practice before trading with real money.

Measure your return on investment

The most important thing about investing is the return.

You can try comparing your stock trading returns to indices such as the S&P 500 (often used as the direction of the overall market), the Nasdaq Composite (used primarily by investors in tech stocks), or other indices based on different industries and geographies to see how your investment returns are performing.

If you find that your returns are not outperforming the index, investing in a low-cost index fund or ETF can be a better choice.

Basically, index funds and ETFs are a combination of multiple stocks, and the performance of index funds is also closely related to the index, which means that if you invest in index funds or ETFs, the performance will be better than your own investment portfolio.

Don't follow suit

To be a successful investor, you don't have to think about finding untapped stocks with potential before anyone else. In fact, when you hear that a stock is going to skyrocket, thousands of professional traders may already be there.

Rather than always be one step behind others, look for investments that will bring value to shareholders over the long term.

You can make active trading a hobby, not necessarily the only way to get rich.

What order types are traded?

Generally speaking, there are 13 different transaction order types for trading stocks. Common ones include market order, limit order, stop loss, day order, and valid until cancelled. Good-till-cancelled GTC orders, GTT (Good Till Trigger), trailing stops and bracket orders, Immediately Fill or Cancel (IOC) order, etc.

Market order

Market order A market order is an order to buy or sell a stock at the current best available price in the market. Market orders are usually guaranteed to be filled, but not at the specified price. Market orders are optimal when the primary goal is immediate trade execution.

Limit order

Limit order A limit order is an order to execute after the price reaches the limit price or better.

Stop loss A stop-limit order is another great tool to limit your potential losses on a trade. This type of order allows you to set stop and limit prices.

Day order

•

Good-till-cancelled GTC orders

A Good Until Cancellation Order (GTC) is an instruction that a trade should remain pending until it is executed or manually cancelled.

- **GTT (Good Till Trigger)** A feature known as GTT (Good Till Trigger) enables customers to make buy or sell orders for any stock at the market or limit price. Once the market price of the stock hits your trigger price, which is the price you specified in the GTT Order, these orders are executed (triggered). Orders from GTT are good for a year.

- **Trailing stops and bracket orders**A trailing stop order allows investors to create an order to limit the maximum loss of an open position without limiting the profit.

- **Bracket orders** are designed to help you limit losses or lock in profits by "bracketing" an order with two orders in opposite directions. When the main order is executed, both sub-orders in opposite directions are activated but only one of the two orders can be triggered. When a child order is triggered, the other child order will be cancelled immediately. The main buy order is "bracketed" by a sell high limit order to lock in profits and a sell low stop order to limit losses. The main sell order is "bracketed" by a buy stop high order to limit the loss and a buy low limit order to lock in the profit.

- **Immediately fill or cancel (IOC)** An Immediately Fill or Cancel (IOC) order states that any portion of the order that is not immediately filled must be cancelled.

Can I borrow money from a broker to buy stocks?

Yes, we call it a margin.

However, this method of investing in stocks is relatively risky. If your trades don't go in the direction you expect, you risk putting yourself in debt.

How to short stocks?

If you decide to trade stocks on margin, you can short the stock.

Shorting a stock is when the stock falls or crashes, and you make money. However, shorting stocks is risky, and you may accidentally end up in debt instead of making money.

What is a market maker?

A market maker is a company or individual that implements stock trading. Market makers connect both ends of the market, providing bid and ask prices for both parties to trade.

Whenever you buy or sell a stock, your order goes through almost every major stock exchange market maker.

What is the difference between a brokerage and an investment bank?

Investment banks are financial intermediaries that provide a wide variety of services. Major investment banks include JPMorgan Chase, Goldman Sachs, Morgan Stanley, Citigroup, Bank of America, Credit Suisse and Deutsche Bank. Deutsche Bank).

If you are very rich, you may be able to trade directly with investment banks.

Otherwise, most people trade through brokerages, and these brokers trade with investment banks on your behalf.

How do I pay tax on trading stocks?

If you want to be an active stock trader, you should pay attention to whether the tax rules for each position are different.

In the U.S., the shorter you hold stock, the more tax you'll have to pay to the IRS. The IRS does this to encourage long-term investing rather than short-term speculation.

If you buy and sell stocks regularly, you may find yourself inadvertently breaking the IRS wash-sale rule. A fake buyback is when you sell a stock and then buy the same or similar stock shortly after. In the United States, you may receive a tax penalty for this.

So remember, if you want to actively traded stocks frequently, remember to do your tax planning first.

CHAPTER FIVE

START TRADING

How to start trading stocks for the first time?

No matter what type of stock trader you are, the following tips can help you make sure you get it right the first time:

- Build your position gradually and slowly.
- You don't need to make a big one at a time, and buying slowly (through strategies such as dollar cost averaging or buy in thirds) can help reduce the risk of price volatility.
- Ignore rumors and advocacy from unknown sources.
- Those forums or sites that receive sponsored ads are not your friends, mentors, or Wall Street gurus. A lot of times they are a pump and dump scam group.
- They buy stocks that no one has heard of and trade in small volumes (usually "penny stocks") and hype them online. When unwitting investors bought the shares and pushed the price higher, they sold the shares for their profits.
- Don't help them grow their pockets. If you're looking for a mentor, you can read the stories of truly successful

people and hear their common sense advice and opinions.

- Maintain good tax records. Keeping good tax records can help you avoid penalties in the future. Another possible benefit is that if the investment loses money,
- Choose your trading partner wisely. To trade stocks, you need a broker, but don't pick just any broker. Choose a brokerage that best matches your investing style and experience.
- For active traders, you should priorities low commissions and fast order execution. For starters, you can find brokerages that offer many educational articles, tutorials, seminars, and trading aids.

Other factors to consider include whether the broker offers the stock analysis tools you want, the quality and availability of the tools, the ease of the platform and customer service, etc.

Regardless, as long as you enjoy the process and don't invest more than you can afford, the time you spend learning the basics of stocks and practicing them will be worth it.

Why trade stock CFDs?

Trading stocks through derivatives gives individuals the flexibility to choose long and short positions. Whether the market is up or down, you can take advantage of profit opportunities without actually owning the underlying asset.

When you trade stocks with leveraged products such as CFDs, you only need to put in a fraction of your total market exposure (called "margin") to open a position. This type of trading can greatly increase the attractiveness of stock trading because it requires only a small amount of up-front capital. It is important to note that while leverage has clear trading advantages, it also comes with risks, as profit and loss are calculated based on the full value of the position, not the guaranteed amount required to open the position.

Risks of trading stocks

Due to leverage (which magnifies the amount of your profits and losses), the risks of stock trading vary widely. Because your profit and loss are calculated based on the full value of the position, not the margin required to open the position.

However, traders can manage risk by using tools. For example, a "stop loss" function allows you to set an exit point in an unfavorable market move, while a "limit" order helps you close a position when the market moves a predetermined amount in a favorable direction.

What are the types of stocks?

Shares listed on the exchange are divided into two categories: common stock and preferred stock. Holding common stock means shareholders have voting rights at general meetings and dividend rights, while preferred stock generally does not carry voting rights, but preferred stockholders have better income conditions than common stockholders.

Will shareholders get a profit?

Yes, but there is no guarantee that such benefits will always be available. Shareholders can generally benefit from their holdings in two ways: dividends and share price appreciation.

Dividends refer to the cash distribution of the company's profits, and the company will regularly distribute them according to the current number of shares held by shareholders.

Bulls and Bears

What do bull and bear markets have to do with the stock market? Bull and bear markets refer to market conditions, whether their value is increasing or decreasing. The market goes up one day and goes down the next. These are called market swings, and they are part of how the whole system works. Bull and bear markets are two symbols that have long been associated with the stock market. A bear market is a market in which the value of a stock falls over a period of time, and a bull market is a market in which the price of a stock rises over a period of time. Usually, the two alternates, and in general, normal bull markets tend to last longer than bear markets.

Major market indices (the plural form of index) track the performance of a group of stocks. These indices are used to represent the movements of a particular stock exchange (such as the TSX NYSE NSE or BSE) and can be referenced when the market is rising or falling. Indices are designed to measure the weighted average of a group of securities.

Some of the major indexes include the TSX Composite, the Dow Jones Industrial Average (DJIA), the S&P 500, nifty50 Sensex and the Nasdaq Composite. When an index falls, it means that the average value of all stocks in that index is lower than the previous trading day.

CHAPTER SIX

STOCK EXCHANGES

Common stock exchanges

The size of a stock exchange is directly related to the number and size of companies listed on the exchange. Below are the most prominent US Indian and Canadian stock exchanges.

- **NSE (National Stock Exchange)** The National Stock Exchange of India (NSE) is a stock exchange. It was established in November 1992. It is the largest stock exchange in India and the third largest in the world in terms of trading volume (second only to the New York Stock Exchange and Nasdaq exchanges). NSE consists of a series of major Indian financial institutions, banks, insurance companies and other financial intermediaries, but operates as a separate entity with ownership.

In 2005, the total number of NSE VSAT terminals was 2799, covering more than 320 cities in India. In March

2006, the total share capital of the NSE market was 438.077 billion Indian rupees, making it the second-largest stock market in South Asia.

- **BSE (Bombay Stock Exchange)** The oldest stock exchange in Asia, the Bombay Stock Exchange (BSE) was established as an association in 1875 and has been known as the BSE for the past 133 years, the first stock exchange in India. The BSE is a place to trade stocks and funds, building up its own country's capital economy market. The BSE index known as SENSEX is India's first stock market index. Apart from being a financial pillar, BSE is also one of Mumbai's most recognizable historic buildings.
- **TSX (Toronto Stock Exchange)** is located in Toronto, Canada. It is the 9th largest exchange in the world by market capitalization. Numerous companies from Canada and around the world are listed on the exchange.
- **NYSE (New York Stock Exchange)** is an American stock exchange located in the financial district of Lower Manhattan in New York City. It is the largest stock exchange in the world in terms of market capitalization of companies listed on the exchange, with dozens of daily occurrences. a billion transactions.
- **NASDAQ (National Association of Securities Dealers Automated Quotations)** is a United States-based electronic marketplace focused on high-tech public companies. It is the second-largest stock exchange in terms of market capitalization of stocks traded, behind the New York Stock Exchange.

What is a brokerage business?

A brokerage firm is a financial institution that acts as an intermediary (or broker). They help investors buy and sell stocks by working with buyers and sellers. Investors can trade in a variety of ways. You can place buy and sell orders via phone, web or app. Most brokerage firms charge per transaction.

There are two main types of brokerage firms, full-service investment brokers and concessional investment brokers (Discount brokers).

Full-Service brokers are known for providing a diverse range of financial services, usually assigning one advisor to each client. In some cases, they are also able to provide additional financial services, including planning services, financial advisory services, wealth management and fiduciary services. They can offer direct investing (or online investing) services, providing self-directed investors with online market research, online education and access to a range of direct trading platforms. It's worth noting that higher levels of service usually mean higher prices.

Discount brokers are a good mid-point option for those who want to get involved in investing but are wary of going it alone. Discount brokers do not provide clients with any investment advice and do not invest gradually. However, if you know what you're doing, a discount broker will act on your behalf, buying and selling stocks and trading options. A full-service broker, on the other hand, will advise you when to buy, when to sell, and how to allocate your investment funds. Some discount brokers do offer monthly newsletters with recommendations printed in them, but this is not a standard service and should not be expected.

CHAPTER SEVEN

INVESTING

An investment is an investment in a business by acquiring securities or directly from an enterprise (enterprises) in order to obtain additional profit or influence the affairs of an enterprise or company. Investments can be classified according to several criteria. Depending on the object of investment, they can be:

- speculative - the purchase of currency, securities, shares, etc., and after an increase in the price of them - the sale and receipt of income due to the difference in value;
- financial - the creation of cash accounts and profit from financial transactions on the stock exchanges;
- venture - investing in new companies or projects with the potential for significant growth;
- real - buying real estate, business, etc.

According to the investment period, investments are:

- short-term - up to 1 year;
- medium-term - from 1 year to 5 years;
- long-term - more than 5 years.

According to the level of risk, investments are divided into:

- on conservative - low;
- moderate - medium;
- aggressive - high.

Investments can be made in various ways:

self-financing - completely at the expense of own funds;

credit financing is the receipt of funds for investments by means of a loan or a loan (in practice, this method is the most common);

equity financing is raising funds for investment by selling company shares;

leasing - with this method, money for investments is received by pledging property.

Why invest?

Whether you're saving for retirement, housing, education, or your future, investing can help you grow your money. If you put your money in a savings account, you may not earn enough interest to beat inflation.

Knowing some investing basics can help you lay the groundwork, so you can set financial goals and determine what types of investments can help you achieve those goals.

Basically, there are **two purposes.**

One is to resist inflation, so that the money you have worked so hard to earn will not shrink, and the **second** is to gain a certain value-added.

So that money can work for me. But as long as the investment will face the problem of risk, the popular explanation, the risk is the possibility that the investor suffers the loss.

Generally divided into two types of risks,

systematic risk and unsystematic risk

Systematic risk :

Systematic risk comes from the entire macro level, including the entire market risk, interest rate risk, exchange rate risk, policy risk and so on. Systemic risk cannot be dispersed among the same assets, and must be offset by combining different assets with each other.

For example, when inflation comes, you must increase the allocation ratio of commodities. Otherwise, if you only allocate stocks, it will be difficult to eliminate the risk of inflation.

Unsystematic risk:

Unsystematic risk: Another type of risk is called unsystematic risk, which is a microscopic risk, such as the risk of thundering corporate performance and financial fraud.

To eliminate this risk, you don't need to cross assets, you only need to match some more varieties.

For example, if you allocate 20 stocks, even if there is a company whose performance is thundering and falls by half, you will only lose 2%. So, what risk you want to eliminate determines how you want to allocate your assets.

If inflation is not a concern, then of course there is no need to configure commodities. The risk of recession is also small, and even bonds can be underweight. Just need to be in the middle of the stock, the diversity selection will do.

Wealth growth will be difficult at the beginning, because your base is small, and it will give you 10-20% of income, which does not seem to quench your thirst, but there is a miracle in the world called compound interest, as long as you can persist in this income, he will let you In the back, the gains are getting higher and higher. And a difference of 1 point can make a lot of difference.

For example, if you want to invest in a 50-year cycle, with an annualization of 10%, your principal will increase by 117 times, but if it is annualized by 12%, it will eventually increase by 289 times, and the latter is 2.5 times of the former. The gap is huge. But in a certain year, the difference is not much.

Banking and insurance sometimes trick you, deliberately confuse simple interest and compound interest, and tell you a high rate of return, but it is actually simple interest calculation, such as 10% per year, if simple interest calculation, then it will only turn over in 10 years. 1 time, only 5 times in 50 years, and 117 times of compound interest, which is more than 20 times of income. Conversely, the annualized rate of simple interest is 10%, and in terms of compound interest, it is only equivalent to an annualized rate of 3.6%, so think about how big a pit this is. Someone said to give you a product with an annual rate of 10%, you must ask whether it is simple interest or compound interest.

In view of the strong late-stage value-added ability of compound interest, we are required to do two things. One is to invest as early as possible, and you must have enough time to roll the snowball. You won't have a lot of trial and error time. Although some people invest at the age of 20, but they still lose money at the age of 40, and still haven't found the right direction, then their future income will be relatively limited.

If you do a questionnaire survey, almost all investors will tell you that he is a stable investor, but in reality, many people have moved towards high-risk aggressive investment. The main reason is that many people are not correct.

You don't even know how much your risk tolerance is. Some people often say in a bull market, I can take 40% of the risk of retracement, but often in a bear market, he can't even hold 10%. Why is this? Because there is good news in a bull market, and he only thinks about it. Retrace 40% of the psychological impact on yourself.

But once in a bear market, it's all bad news, except for the stock market falling, it will scare you every day. I tell you that you can't do it, run away, and your mentality will collapse faster. So, this illusion can make it easy for you to ignore your own risk management.

At present, there are several logics in investment, one is fundamental analysis, the other is technical analysis, and there is an efficient market hypothesis, which tells you to hold the index. But in fact, the most basic logic is two points, timing and stock selection, or asset selection. Generally,

There are several investment methods of operation.

First method:

First methodis to believe that both timing and stock selection are feasible. The more incompetent and inexperienced investors are, the more confident they are. They generally choose this way, based on their own judgement, to invest.

Second method:

Second method is to believe in the timing, not in the choice of assets. Generally, technical analysis is done in this way. Only in the stage of strong rise, buy low and sell high, and strive to achieve bottom-hunting and top-escape.

Third method:

Third methodConversely, value investors who do not believe in timing but believe in assets are usually in this category. They will hold heavy positions in undervalued assets in an attempt to cross the cycle and achieve market-beating returns.

Fourth method:

Fourth method Simply think that the market is efficient, I can't do it for you, so it's basically a capital service, allocate your money to several types of assets in proportion, and then do nothing, let these assets go up by themselves, anyway. No matter what cycle, you always have something that can go up. For example, the asset allocation we are talking about is this category. I told you about the simplest permanent investment portfolio of Harry Brown, 25% cash,

25% bonds, 25% stocks and 25% commodity gold, corresponding to the four cycles of recession, recovery, stagflation and overheating respectively. If you want to beat the market, then choose the first three methods. If you do not want to beat the market, but also do not want to be beaten by the market, and want to make money steadily, you choose the fourth method.

fifth method:

fifth method which is some of the asset allocation methods at the selected time, that is, we will act only when we have absolute certainty, and obtain excess returns by adjusting the combination ratio. , most of the time, basically not moving. This method can ensure that we will not be beaten by the market, but we can occasionally make some extra money, so the returns are higher than simple asset allocation. Of course, the requirements will also be higher. We need to understand market sentiment fluctuations, understand the cycle selection of the market, and know the valuation of the market well. These requirements are actually quite high. If investors are not careful, it is likely that they will make the first one. They choose both the time and the asset, and finally lose money.

In modern finance, people like Markowitz defined the capital asset pricing model, which is taught in many universities, and he believes that returns and risks can be determined by formulas, so how much risk you can bear, the formula will give How much income do you match, and then based on these, you can find the corresponding asset portfolio and hold it all the time. Markowitz also became the father of modern portfolio theory.

Of course, the calculation formula is still quite complicated, and it requires a strong mathematical foundation to understand it. He calculates the correlation between stocks to obtain the correlation, and puts unrelated assets together to obtain a risk-return rate. thus, forming a combination. Unless you are a professional actuary, there is no need to understand the calculation method.

I only need the results, and our dedicated partners will calculate the results and select stocks and funds. Most investment managers don't actually count this, as long as they know how to use it.

Now there is another popular investment method, which is **behavioral finance.**

The things you are rushing to buy must be expensive, and the things you are rushing to sell will be sold out. Cheaper, the higher the degree of market consensus expectations, the higher the winning rate in the opposite direction. Everyone thinks that if the stock market is going to rise sharply, it may not take long for the stock market to fall, and it may still fall sharply. But investors are also prone to mistakes. It is easy to take the group sample around him as a large sample. When everyone around him is bullish, he feels that all investors in the market are bullish.

So, there is a deviation of the law of decimals, and finally the probability is wrongly estimated. There are many ways to avoid this situation, that is, be sure to look at the changes in volume. No matter how many people are bullish, and the trading volume is not enlarged, it means that these are not enough to believe. In behavioral finance, more problems are pointed out, such as overconfidence, prospect theory, anchoring effect, confirmation bias, etc. These are all places where it is very easy to make mistakes.

Next, let's take a look at the assets we come into contact with in life, such as houses, cars, jewelry, watches, stocks, deposits, and financial management that are regarded as assets in everyone's impression. But from the perspective of investment, good assets must have an effect, that is, it can bring in the inflow of cash, that is, if you buy a goose, it will lay eggs, and it will keep the money close to you instead of away from you.

If you use this standard to judge, obviously A car is not a good asset, it will depreciate continuously after it is bought, and you have to put a lot of money on it, such as insurance, gas, parking, maintenance and so on. So, by analogy, jewelry and watches are also not good assets. Second-hand ones will definitely depreciate, and the liquidity is very poor, so it is difficult for you to sell them. So, in the end, from the perspective of asset allocation, the assets we can actually use, that is, stocks, bonds, commodities, real estate, and cash, these are more pragmatic assets. Tomorrow we will look at the performance of these assets separately.

Why is investing better than saving?

"Is the money enough to spend?" If we ask this question, our first reaction may be not enough money.

There are many reasons why it will not be enough, one of which is the decline in purchasing power caused by inflation, that is, our money is depreciating in value. Many people who don't want to worry about financial management always think that it's good to put money in a fixed deposit, with fixed interest every year, and you don't need to be busy with financial management, why not? The "real purchasing power" of money decreases. When the annual inflation rate is higher than the fixed deposit rate, it means that the value of money has shrunk.

In fact, inflation has always existed, and wealth is shrinking day by day, so don't think that putting your money in the bank will be fine. We can strive to preserve the value of our wealth through investment and financial management.

Investments hold the key to an investor's future. They help bridge the gap between their dreams and reality. Here are some of the benefits of investing*:

To achieve your financial goals Whether it's buying a house or buying a car, paying for your child's education or wedding, or even planning your retirement, investing can help you achieve your financial goals and objectives. Investing your capital is the most optimal way to achieve your long-term goals.

To defeat inflation, investing your money also helps you fight inflation. If you choose not to invest and keep your money in a regular savings account, the purchasing power of your money could decline over time due to inflation. So, to ensure your money's worth, it makes sense to invest in financial products that have the potential to earn returns above inflation.

To Earn Significant Returns, Investment avenues such as stocks or mutual funds** have the potential to generate significantly higher returns than a savings account or bank term deposits.

Why invest in the stock market?

The most obvious reason to consider investing in the stock market is for long-term capital appreciation. You can also support other companies to grow and support the economy as a whole.

While it takes time to understand the stock market and how it works, once you do, technology can easily contribute to your own financial portfolio. By investing, you can also improve your financial literacy.

Of course, investing in the stock market also has risks. You really need to educate yourself and invest wisely.

How to start investing?

Introduction to Investing for Newbies.

Investing in stocks is a great way to grow your wealth.

In India, or the United States, the wealthier people, the higher the proportion of their assets invested in the stock market.

For investors with a long-term investment objective, stocks are a great way to invest, even during times of market volatility. The stock market crashes we've seen in 2020 also means you have the opportunity to buy stocks at a cheaper price.

When you're just starting out investing in stocks, you may not know where to start, but I assure you it's actually quite simple.

And you don't necessarily have to be like the legendary Warren Buffett to be a successful investor, anyone -- no matter your age or wealth -- has the chance to be a successful investor.

The legendary Warren Buffett defined investing as "...a process of raising money now, with the hope of getting more money in the future."

As a newbie in the investing world, you have a lot of questions, and your first question is probably: How do I start investing? What is the best strategy for investing?

Before learning how to start investing, you can start by understanding what type of investor you are.

What kind of investor are you?

Before investing, you can ask yourself:

- What type of investor am I?
- What kind of investment product is right for me?

This reminds me of a story shared by an American writer, Doug who was a trader at a brokerage.

He said he was a rookie trader at the company at the time. One day he received a new client who wanted to buy gold mining stocks, and as usual, he chatted with the client about some related topics and helped him buy the stocks he wanted.

The next morning, he received a call from a client.

"I want to sell all my stocks right now!"

His friend was puzzled because the client's holdings had barely changed. He asked, "What made you want to sell all your stock?"

"Because I saw some negative news, I want to sell it all!"

Clients don't know how the stock market works. His friend explained to the client that there was no way he could sell the stock right away (especially since there weren't as many people trading gold mining stocks), but the client insisted on selling all of his holdings right away.

Later, his friend said, "Otherwise, I'll buy your stock."

After sending the client away, his friend said it was the first time he had bought a stock with great potential in the future at the cheapest price.

Some people can be very stressful about investing, while others may never get used to it. Some investors like to actively participate in the management of their funds, while others like to "leave the funds alone".

Most importantly, you need to know yourself before investing.

CHAPTER EIGHT

HOW DO I START INVESTING?

1. Decide on your investment preferences

Before investing, you can first understand your preferences. You are:

"I like to do everything myself, and I think learning to invest is very interesting!" Or

"Know the benefits of investing, but hope someone can help manage it."

If you like to do it yourself, you can find a lot of useful information in this book.

If you prefer others to help you manage, you can find an investment trust or asset management company, or use a robo-advisor. You can also find a lot about this type of service in this blog.

The robo-advisor will help you automatically allocate and build your investment portfolio in the stock and bond markets with software based on your investment goals. Not only are robo-advisors low-cost, they can also help you optimize your taxes. Almost all major brokerages offer such a service.

2. Set your investment goals

Next, you can take a moment to think about what your investment goals are.

How much money do you hope to get by investing, and when do you hope to achieve this goal?

Generally, we divide investment objectives into 2 categories:

Long-term goals:

The most common long-term goal is retirement. Other long-term goals include making a down payment on a home, paying your tuition, or wanting to buy your dream vacation home in 10 years' time and go on an anniversary trip of a lifetime.

Short-term goals:

Short-term investment goals include next year's vacation, the car you want to buy next year, etc.

For new investors, I would recommend establishing a long-term investment goal first. Wait until you become more familiar with investing before establishing short-term investment goals that suit your preferences.

3. Know your investment options (stocks, bonds, mutual funds, ETFs, trusts, etc.)

It is important to understand each financial instrument and its risks. Popular investments include:

Stock:

Stock is the ownership of shares in a company.

The price of the stock depends on the company and can range from single digits to several thousand dollars. For starters, you might consider buying stocks through mutual funds. More on mutual funds to come.

Bond:

Basically, a bond is a loan to a company or government that repays your money over a certain number of years. While waiting for repayment, you will receive interest.

Investing in bonds is generally less risky than stocks because you can know when companies and governments will repay and how much money you can make. But bonds have lower long-term yields, which is why they are usually only a small part of long-term investment portfolios.

Mutual Fund:

A mutual fund can be said to be a portfolio that combines a variety of different stocks and bonds.

Mutual funds save you the trouble of picking stocks and bonds yourself, and you can buy a diverse portfolio with just one trade. Because of this, mutual funds are less risky than buying individual stocks.

Some mutual funds are managed by professionals, but index funds (a type of mutual fund) follow the performance of a specific stock market index (such as the S&P 500). Because index funds do not require professionals to manage like mutual funds, index funds have lower fees than mutual funds.

ETF Exchange Traded Fund:

ETFs exchange-traded funds, like mutual funds, tie together many single investments. Where it differs is that ETFs are traded throughout the day like stocks, and are bought in the form of share prices.

ETF share prices are usually lower than the minimum investment requirements of mutual funds, making them a good choice for those who are new to investing or have a small budget.

For starters, you can start with the financial instruments mentioned above. Of course, there are many other financial instruments and ways to invest, and if you're already familiar with stocks, bonds, mutual funds, and ETFs.

4. Select a broker and open an account

Most stocks, bonds, funds and other investment products can be purchased through brokerage accounts. Banks also usually offer a variety of different types of investment accounts, such as savings accounts, foreign exchange accounts, etc.

When choosing a brokerage and opening an account, you should not only check whether the brokerage provides the products and services you want to invest in, but also pay attention to the brokerage's fees, such as transaction fees, minimum deposit restrictions, etc. If your investment goal is retirement, some brokerages may offer tax benefits specifically for that goal.

5. Develop your investment strategy

Now that the account is open, you can start formulating your investment strategy.

If your investment goal is more than 20 years old (for example, your investment goal is retirement), then you may consider putting your money into the stock market. But picking specific stocks can be complicated and time-consuming, and if you don't have that much time, buying stocks through lower-cost mutual funds, index funds, or ETFs may be a better option.

If your goals are short-term, say you want to reach your investment goal within 5 years, you may want to consider options other than stocks. If you don't want to take too much risk, you can put your money in a safe savings account, asset management account, or a low-risk investment portfolio.

If you are willing to take greater risk, you can achieve your short-term investment goals by investing in options, futures and foreign exchange, or other alternative investments (such as cryptocurrencies). Be careful, though, these markets are much more risky than the stock market, so it is best to understand the risks of these financial instruments and alternative investments before investing your money.

CHAPTER NINE

GET STARTED NOW

Finally, don't forget to get started right away. The earlier you invest, the better your chances of benefiting.

Why? Because of compound interest.

Compound interest can snowball your account balance.

Suppose you invest $200 or 15,977.05 Indian Rupee a month for 10 years and your average annual return is 6%. At the end of ten years, you'll have an income of $33,300 (26,60,178.83 Indian Rupee). Of this amount, $24,200(19,32,979.84 Indian Rupee) is your contribution, and $9,100(7,26,864.32 Indian Rupee) is the interest you earned on your investment.

Sure, the stock market has its ups and downs, but the sooner you invest, the more time you have to get out of trouble if you're in trouble -- and the more time you have for your money to grow.

In addition to compounding interest, the sooner you invest, the better you will be able to keep you out of inflation. What was available for a few coins 20 years ago may no longer be available. Inflation is quietly changing our living standards, so investing is best done early.

How to Invest Your Money in the Stock Market

When thinking about how to invest,

- what is the first thing that comes to your mind?
- Is it the excitement of discovering a stock that you think could be profitable?
- Are you hesitant about how to start investing?
- Is it that success in other areas of your life that gives you the confidence to want to conquer new things?

You've done your research on the stock market, and now you're ready to invest. The first decision you will make is whether to invest as a self-directed investor or with the help of an advisor.

Whether you invest on your own or have a financial advisor to help you achieve your investment goals, the more you know, the better you can make informed decisions.

Learning how to invest can mean different things to different people. It unleashes your limitless potential and ignites dreams you didn't even realize you had. When you take charge of your investments, you may be inspired by the skills you can learn and the goals you can achieve.

From $5,000 to $22 Million:

Everyone knows the Warren Buffett legend, but not many people know the low-key Annie Scheiber.

Buffett started buying stocks at the age of 11, and Annie's life was the same as most of us - growing up ordinary, then getting a life and a job.

She never made more than $3,100 a year, was never promoted, and retired with only $5,000 in all her life savings.

However, after she retired in 1944, she turned her life savings from $5,000 to $22 million by investing in stocks.

Although in the 1930s, all her friends shunned the stock market because of the Wall Street crash, she managed to manage her own portfolio.

Before her death, no one other than her lawyer and stockbroker knew that Anne was such a successful investor.

This history tells us that you don't need to be like Buffett for anyone to have a chance to be a successful investor.

How to start investing in stocks?

1. Decide how you want to invest in stocks

There are several ways to invest in stocks. First, you can decide which one of the following is more suitable for your preference:

"I like to DIY everything, and I think picking stocks is fun!"

"I know investing in stocks is good, but I hope someone can help me manage it."

If you like "do it yourself", you can find a lot of information in the following articles and this blog.

If you prefer someone else to help you manage, you might consider using a robo-advisor.

Robo-advisors provide low-cost and convenient asset management services, which are provided by almost all major brokerages. Robo-advisors help you automatically allocate your portfolio based on your investment goals.

Once you've decided on your preferred method, you can start opening an account with a brokerage.

2. Open an investment account

Usually to invest in stocks you need to open an investment account.

People who like to manage their investments themselves, you need to open a brokerage account. For those who want someone else to manage their investments for you, you can choose to open an account through a robo-advisor.

Investing in U.S. or Indian stocks can be done by opening an account online.

Whether it's a brokerage or a robo-advisor, there are usually very low minimum capital limits.

I want to do it myself

You can choose a brokerage account that operates on the Internet, because such an account is most likely to provide you with the fastest and cheapest way to buy stocks (especially US and Indian stocks), bonds, funds and various investment products.

When opening an account with a broker you need to be aware of the costs (like commissions for trades, account fees, etc.), what investments you have access to (like if you like funds, does the broker offer you the best ETF options) and does any broker offer research and tools that you might use.

DIY investing

Do-it-yourself (DIY) investing refers to a method of investing where you manage your own portfolio through a full-blown trading platform or a simplified goal-based application.

Some of the reasons why you might consider independently managing your investments as a self-directed investor are as follows:

- Fees are lower.
- The freedom to make investment decisions on your own time.
- More control over your capital appreciation.
- Flexibility to choose from a wide range of investment vehicles.

Other factors to consider include investment knowledge level, amount of money available for DIY investing, and risk tolerance.

We can help you with a wide range of teaching resources, tools, market information and research, and insights.

I want someone else to help me manage

A robo-advisor saves you from having to pick and choose which stocks or funds to buy.

Robo-advisors provide you with comprehensive investment management: these companies will ask you what your investment goals are, and then automatically help you build a portfolio that meets your investment goals.

This service may sound expensive, but its management fee is actually much cheaper than that of a human asset management service or an advisor – usually robo-advisors charge 0.25% of account funds as a fee.

3. Understand the difference between stocks and stock mutual funds

For most people, investing in the stock market represents investing in either of the following types:

Equity mutual funds or ETF exchange-traded funds.

These funds allow you to buy a variety of different stocks at the same time in one purchase. Index funds and ETFs are a type of mutual fund that tracks an index. For example, an S&P 500 index fund replicates the index by buying stocks of companies in the S&P 500. Investing in this fund means you own a fraction of the shares of these companies. You can buy several different funds to build a diversified and diverse portfolio.

Individual stocks.

If you particularly like a company or think it has potential, you can start investing by buying one or more shares of that company. You can also build a diversified portfolio yourself by buying individual stocks, but usually you will need more capital and a lot of research to do it successfully.

The benefit of a stock mutual fund is that it is inherently diversified, which means less risk. But the disadvantage of a mutual fund is that it is less likely to rise like individual stocks.

The beauty of buying individual stocks is that if you pick them well, your returns may be substantial, but at the same time the odds of individual stocks making you rich are low.

For most investors -- especially those investing in retirement pensions -- the safest and most reasonable option is a mutual fund.

4. Set a budget for your stock investment

Beginners usually have 2 questions:

- How much money do I need to start investing in stocks?
- How much you need depends on the price of the stock (stocks can range from a few dollars to several thousand dollars).

If you have a low budget and want to buy mutual funds, ETFs are your best bet. Usually mutual funds have a minimum limit of $1,000, but ETFs trade like stocks.

This means that you will buy the ETF at the stock price, sometimes below $100.

How much should I invest in the stock market?

If you want to buy stocks through mutual funds, especially if your investment goals are long-term, you can allocate most of your funds to the stock market.

In the U.S., a 30-year-old investor investing for retirement might put 80% of his portfolio in stock mutual funds and the rest in bond funds.

Individual stocks are another matter. Unless you are very confident in your ability to pick stocks and build a portfolio, I would recommend investing no more than 10% in individual stocks.

5. *Get started investing*

The stock investing environment is full of intricate strategies and methodologies, but there are also many investors who have succeeded in investing with only basic knowledge.

Usually, mutual funds can be very successful to make up the majority of your portfolio. Warren Buffett famously said, "A cheap S&P 500 index fund is the best investment for most Americans."

CHAPTER TEN

PLAN BEFORE INVESTING

Planning time horizons, risk levels, investment objectives and account types can help make your personal investing process smoother. Before researching different types of investments, ask yourself the following questions:

How long will you invest?

Determining the time frame depends on your financial goals and how long after you have invested the money you will need to use it. When investing for long-term goals like retirement, you might consider reinvesting your returns to help compound each year -- which could accelerate your money's growth in value.

How much risk can you take?

Your risk tolerance can be classified as conservative, moderate or aggressive. Your risk tolerance can determine which type of investment you choose. For example, if you have short-term goals, you might consider lower-risk investments (conservative). In terms of long-term goals, your tolerance for market volatility may be higher (aggressive).

What is your goal?

Before you start making an investment decision, you should keep a clear goal in mind. Consider your lifestyle and the fact that your goals may change over time. For example, your goal today might be to put $X into your Registered Retirement Savings Plan (RRSP) or save for a specific purchase. Life is fickle, priorities change, and so do your goals.

Which account types meet your different needs?

Once you have determined your financial goals, you can choose from different types of accounts to achieve your savings goals.

For investment and financial management in the United States, and India.

what types of investment accounts and investment channels are there?

For investment and financial management in the **United States**, the most commonly mentioned investment in stocks is probably stock investment. In fact, in the United States, there are of course many investment methods besides stocks. Investment pipeline.

There are 4 ways to buy stocks in the US:

1. Direct stock purchase plans (DSPPs)
2. Purchase through your retirement account (401K, IRA, Roth IRA, etc.)
3. Through a brokerage (Brokerage/Broker)
4. Through a bank

Direct stock purchase plans (DSPPs):

For the general public, which can save intermediate brokerage fees (but there may still be some costs incurred, subject to company regulations), but not every company All provide this service, you can find the official website of the company you are interested in by yourself. The funds in the retirement account can be invested in stocks. The advantage is that the capital gains tax can be saved, but the retirement account cannot be withdrawn at any time.

Individual Retirement Account:

If a small company doesn't have a 401K in its benefit plan, consider an IRA, another type of individual retirement account that you can open yourself. Note that an IRA is not an investment commodity, but an account of investment. Roth IRAs and traditional IRAs are the two main types. The main difference is when you need to pay taxes. With a Roth IRA, you pay taxes before you deposit your funds, and don't pay taxes when you withdraw them later. With a traditional IRA, account funds are pre-deposited and tax is paid when withdrawn at a later date.

401(k): Generally, after joining the company, the company HR will provide you with a benefit plan provided by the company, the largest of which is the 401K corporate retirement benefit plan. Fund the account.

Through a brokerage (Brokerage/Broker):

There are so many brokers in the United States that handling fees, reliability and service are definitely the most important aspects for investors. Brokers can be further divided into traditional brokers (full service brokers) and online brokers (online discount service brokers) .

Traditional brokerages:

such as Merrill Lynch, Salomon Smith Barney, Morgan Stanley and Dean Witter, etc., provide professional financial advisors or professional managers to provide customers with consulting, financial planning, advice and order management services, which are usually expensive.

Online brokerages:

Usually, customers make their own investment decisions. The official website will also provide relevant market analysis and tools. Some online brokerages also provide professional financial advisor services (extra charge).

Basically, online brokerage fees are lower than those of traditional brokerage firms or brokers.

Types of Brokerage Accounts

There are three different types of brokerage accounts that can be opened:

•

Individual brokerage account:

Can be opened in the name of only one account owner.

-

Joint brokerage account:

Can be opened in the names of two or more people, typically spouses.

-

Custodial brokerage account:

Can be set up for the benefit of minors under the age of 18. Depending upon the state of residents, these are typically set up as UGMA (Uniform Gift to Minors Act) or UTMA (Uniform Transfers to Minors Act) accounts.

You can also find your own preferred or closer brokers. All U.S. securities firms are regulated by the U.S. Financial Industry Regulatory Authority (FINRA) . Business history and scale of operations to ensure their own interests.

[Non-citizen, non-green card foreigner to open an account] If you live in the United States for temporary reasons (study, OPT, work) or tourism, you should be eligible to open an account, depending on the length of stay and the type of visa, you can contact the broker to determine whether you are eligible qualifications. Even overseas, you can open an account in the US stock market through an online brokerage, and you need to upload and provide document data, including documents such as ID card and passport copy.

Stocks can be purchased from brokers, and you can buy US stocks through the following brokers:

- eToro
- Firstrade
- Interactive Brokers
- Webull
- Futu Moomoo
- Charles Schwab
- E*Trade
- TD Ameritrade
- Fidelity
- Robinhood

You can buy Indian stocks through the following brokers:

- Zerodha
- Upstox
- Groww
- Angel One
- Alice Blue
- Choice Broking
- ICICIdirect
- 5paisa
- Kotak Securities
- HDFC Securities
- IIFL Securities
- Motilal Oswal
- Sharekhan
- SBI Securities
- Paytm Money

- AxisDirect
- Geojit
- Edelweiss
- Religare
- SMC Global

How to Make Money by Investing in Stocks?

It's not hard to buy stocks, but it's a little harder to successfully make money consistently in the stock market. Especially as we see unanticipated events in 2020 that have a huge impact on the stock market, it becomes especially important to know how to prepare for any scenario.

Stock investors usually make money with stocks in the following two ways:

- If the price of the stock rises while holding the stock, investors can sell the stock at a higher price to make a profit.
- Dividend distribution. Dividends are money that a company pays out to shareholders on a regular basis. Not all stocks pay dividends, but those that do are usually quarterly.

Over the past 100 years, the average annual return on the stock market has been 10%.

Usually investing in stocks with a long-term goal, diversification is best. This means that your portfolio can survive in good times and bad.

If you want to invest in individual stocks, you need to spend more time doing research, including a deep understanding of the company's operations and financial conditions.

Many investors choose to invest in stocks through mutual funds, index funds, and ETFs that buy stocks. These funds allow you to buy multiple stocks in a single trade, reducing the risk of a single company stock and saving time in research.

Tips for making money investing in stocks

1. Always check your emotions before investing
2. Pick companies, not stocks
3. Plan ahead, take precautions
4. Build your own stock position with minimal risk
5. Avoid overtrading

1. Always check your emotions before investing

"Successful investing has nothing to do with IQ... What you need is more control over your impulsive temper than others, which in turn gets others into trouble." - Berkshire. Warren Hathaway, chairman of Berkshire Hathaway . Warren Buffett

You should always use your rationality to make investment decisions, not your guts. In fact, emotional overtrading is the most common way investors can hurt their portfolio returns.

It might sound easy, but it's actually very difficult to do. My advice is, whenever you feel you 'need to make a decision right away' - what not to do. Take a step back, take a deep breath, or walk around, give the thought a moment, and then look back to see if you really "need" to make this decision.

If you do, you'll find yourself less and less regretful about your decisions. Even if you find out that you made a mistake, you will know why you made the decision in the first place and learn from it.

2. Pick companies, not stocks

Many people often forget that stocks represent companies, businesses that actually operate in our lives, not just a bunch of numbers. Don't let picking stocks become an abstract concept.

Always remember this: By buying stock in a company, you are a part owner of that company.

You can imagine yourself as an entrepreneur whose goal is to make money by buying and selling businesses. When looking for a business, you naturally want to know how the company works, where it stands in the industry as a whole, who its competitors are, what its future prospects are and whether it can help you in what you already have. Bring something new to the business.

3. Plan ahead and take precautions

Impulsive decision-making can easily lead you to buy high and sell low, feeling like you're forever trailing behind others or failing.

How to overcome this?

I suggest that you can write an investment journal to record your investment behaviour, which will be of great help to you.

You can write down every stock in your portfolio and record why and when you invested in those stocks. Why these stocks are worth investing in, and what else should happen when you should consider selling them.

- **Why do you find a company attractive?**
- **What do you expect the company to look like going forward, and what are your reasons behind it?**
- **Which metrics do you think are important, and what criteria do you use to judge the company's development?**
- **If you want to sell the stock, what are your reasons, and are those reasons good?**

This will help you clear your mind when you are emotionally affected. In 2020, we saw many investors panic. Keeping your investment diary can help you plan ahead in any situation and take precautions.

4. Build your own stock position with minimal risk

Remember, time is your best weapon.

The goal of a successful investor is to be rewarded over the next few years or decades, which means you should spend a little more time picking research when buying stocks. Here are 3 strategies for buying stocks to help you reduce the risk of price volatility.

Dollar-cost average OR Systematic Investment Plan (SIP)

Dollar-cost average or Systematic Investment Plan (SIP) may sound complicated, but it's actually quite simple. Dollar cost averaging or Systematic Investment Plan (SIP) involves the disciplined investment of a certain amount of money at regular intervals, such as weekly or monthly.

When the stock price falls, this amount can buy more shares, and when the stock price rises, you can buy fewer shares. This means that overall, the average price you pay will be stable.

Some online brokerages that trade per share allow you to set up automatic investment schedules.

Buy in thirds

Buy in thirds Like dollar cost averaging or Systematic Investment Plan (SIP), Buy in Thirds can help you avoid buying high and selling land in the first place.

Divide the amount you want to invest by 3, then, as the name suggests, pick 3 points each to buy the stock. These 3 points can be time, such as monthly or quarterly, or they can be selected based on company performance or events.

For example, you can buy stock in a company before a product is released, and if the product is hot, put the next third of your money into it, and if it's not, take the rest of the money elsewhere.

Buy "the basket"

Can't decide which company in an industry will perform well?

Then buy them all. Buying a basket of stocks can reduce the pressure on your selection.

Buying a "basket of stocks" means that if there are winners, you won't miss out; if there are losses, the gains of the winners will offset the losses of the losers. This strategy can also help you find which companies you want to invest in, and then adjust your positions.

One of the things to be aware of is the possibility that the entire industry will not perform well, so you should also understand the prospects of the industry before choosing an industry.

5. Avoid overtrading

I suggest that you check your stock on a quarterly basis - such as when you receive your company's quarterly report.

If you keep an eye on your stock all the time, it can lead you to overreact to short-term events. You may be overly concerned with the stock price rather than the value of the company itself, feeling like you need to do something when you don't have to.

If you notice a large price movement in one of your stocks, your first task is to find out what caused the event. Is it because of a change in the company's basic business? Will it have a significant impact on the company's long-term prospects? Or is it actually just a collateral effect of an unrelated event that is only short-term?

In general, the short-term impact of events has little to do with the long-term performance of a good company, but rather how investors react to these events.

Keep a journal of your investments to help you navigate the stock market successfully.

CHAPTER TWELVE

Types of Investment Accounts in India

As the name suggests, an investment plan is a financial tool that can help you build sustainable wealth for your future needs. There are many investment plans available today that allow you to systematically invest your savings in various money market products and help you reach your financial goals. These investment plans offer the highly desirable advantage of wealth creation through disciplined long-term investments. Today, some of the most popular investment options are:

a) **Unit Linked Insurance Plans (ULIPs)**

b) **Public Provident Funds (PPF)**

c) **Monthly Income Plans**

d) **Mutual funds**

e) **Sukanya Samriddhi Account (SSY)**

f) **Senior Citizen Savings Scheme (SCSS)**

g) Tax saving Fixed Deposits

What are the different types of investments?

There are four main investment or asset classes you can choose from, each with different characteristics, risks and benefits.

Once you're familiar with the different types of assets, you can start thinking about combining assets that suit your individual situation and risk tolerance.

Growth investment

This type of investment is more suitable for long-term investors who are willing and able to withstand market ups and downs.

Growth Investing: Equities

Stocks are considered a growth investment because they help your original investment grow in value over the medium to long term.

If you own the stock, you can also earn income from dividends, which are effectively a portion of a company's profits paid to its shareholders.

Of course, the stock may also be worth less than what you paid for it. Prices can fluctuate on a daily basis, and stocks are generally best for long-term investors who can withstand these ups and downs.

Stocks have historically provided higher returns than other assets and are considered one of the riskiest types of investments.

Growth Investments: Real Estate

Real estate is also considered a growth investment, as the price of houses and other properties can rise substantially over the medium to long term.

However, just like stocks, properties can also depreciate in value and carry the risk of loss.

It can be invested directly through the purchase of real estate, or indirectly through real estate investment funds.

Defensive investment

These investments are more focused on consistently generating income than growth and are considered less risky than growth investments.

Defensive Investing: Cash Investing

Cash investments include everyday bank accounts, high-interest savings accounts, and term deposits.

Of all investment types, they generally have the lowest potential returns.

While they offer no opportunity for capital growth, they can provide regular income that can play an important role in protecting wealth and de-risking a portfolio.

Defensive Investing: Fixed Interest

The most well-known type of fixed-interest investment is bonds, which essentially are governments or corporations borrowing money from investors and paying them interest in return.

Bonds are also considered a defensive investment because they generally offer lower potential returns and a lower level of risk than stocks or real estate.

They can also be sold relatively quickly like cash, though with the caveat that they are not without the risk of capital loss.

Types of investment

There are many types of investments to choose from. Here are 18 common types of investments to help you understand immediately and easily understand the different types of investments, how they work and their risks, so you can start to decide which type of investment is right for you.

The most common types of investments are:

- Stocks
- Bonds
- Mutual Funds
- ETF Exchange Traded Funds (Exchange-Traded Funds)
- Certificate of Deposit
- Retirement Plans
- Options (Options)
- Annuities
- Cryptocurrencies
- Commodities
- Bank Products
- Saving for Education
- Real Estate
- Fixed Deposits

- Public Provident Fund (PPF)
- National Pension System (NPS)
- Unit Linked Insurance Plan (ULIP)
- Senior Citizens' Savings Scheme

Stocks:

Stocks are the most popular and easiest type of investment. When you buy stock in a company, you buy an ownership stake in the company. Many of America's and India's biggest companies -- like Apple, Facebook, Wipro and Infosys-- are public companies, and you can easily buy their shares by opening an account with a brokerage.

You need to be aware of market trends and keep abreast of news about companies you want to buy stocks for investment. You expect the company to pay a decent dividend , or that the company's value rises in the future.

A rise in the value of a company means that the stock price rises, so you can sell the stock at a higher price for a profit. The risk with stocks is that the company you invest in may go bankrupt, meaning your stock will be worthless. But if you are investing in a big company like Apple, Facebook, Amazon, etc., it is usually unlikely that it will go out of business.

Bonds:

When you buy a bond issued by a company or government, you are lending money to the company or government. Bonds issued by companies are called corporate bonds, and bonds issued by local governments are called municipal bonds. Bonds issued by the Treasury are called Treasuries.

Usually bonds have a term, after which you can get your money back, plus the interest on the loan. But bonds may also be traded among investors. Bonds typically offer a much lower rate of return than stocks and are less risky. Bonds also carry certain risks, such as the possibility that the company issuing the bonds may fail, or the government may default. But in general, investors consider government bonds to be a very safe investment.

Mutual Fund:

A mutual fund is a portfolio of stocks and bonds. A mutual fund is an investment scheme that pools the funds of many investors to buy investment commodities. Mutual funds can be actively managed or passively managed. Mutual funds are managed by professionals, and most funds are made up of many types of assets: such as stocks, bonds, and other securities. Actively managed mutual funds are invested in stocks and other investment products selected by the fund manager.

Passive management tracks specific stock market indices (like the Dow Jones Industrial Average, the S&P 500, Nifty50, Sensex, etc), which we call Index Funds.

Some mutual funds invest only in stocks, some only in bonds, and some have a mix of the two.

Because mutual funds invest in stock and bond markets, they share common risks. But because a mutual fund has diversified investment products, its own risk is less than that of a single stock and bond.

ETF Exchange Traded Funds (Exchange-Traded Funds) Index Funds and Index Equity Funds (ETFs):

Exchange-traded funds (ETFs) are similar to mutual funds in that they are a portfolio, the only difference being that ETFs are traded as stocks. ETFs are passively managed funds that invest collectively in diversified securities based on index funds. Investors can freely buy and sell ETFs during the trading day, It is a liquid security that can be traded on stock exchanges throughout the country. While mutual funds, can only see your net investment value after purchasing the fund.

Like mutual funds, ETFs are made up of a number of different investments, such as stocks, bonds, commodities, and currencies, but they trade just like stocks. These funds are highly liquid, as they can be traded on the stock exchange at the request of investors.

Trading prices are determined by market forces and can be traded through the stock exchange during daily business hours. ETFs are often recommended for newcomers to investing because ETFs are more diverse than stocks. You can reduce investment risk by buying ETFs that track the broader market index.

The risks associated with ETFs depend on the type of underlying index. If it is a mid-cap index, it has medium risk. In addition, ETFs have relatively low asset management fees compared to mutual funds.

Certificate of Deposit:

Among many types of investments in India, A certificate of deposit (Certificate of Deposit) is a very low risk investment. A certificate of deposit is when you give the bank a sum of money that you keep for a specific period of time. Once it matures, you can get your principal back, plus interest. Usually, the longer you keep it, the higher your interest will be. CDs are money market instruments issued against money deposited by investors. He invests in the bank in dematerialized form for a fixed period. Certificates of Deposit are issued by the Federal Deposit Insurance Corporation (FDIC) and regulated by the Reserve Bank of India (RBI). There is no major risk in certificates of deposit.

Investing Tips for a CD

A CD can be issued to an issuer for a minimum amount of Rs 10 lakh or more.

The maturity period of certificates of deposit issued by commercial banks ranges from 7 days to 1 year. Given that, certificates of deposit issued by financial institutions have maturity of 1 to 3 years.

Retirement Plans:

There are many types of retirement benefit plans in the **United States**. Employer-sponsored workplace retirement benefit plans include 401(k) and 403(b).

If you don't have a workplace retirement benefit plan, you can choose an individual retirement benefit plan (IRA), including a traditional or Roth plan.

Retirement benefit plans are not a separate investment class in themselves, but an investment vehicle that you can use to buy stocks, bonds, and funds.

The biggest advantage of a retirement benefit plan (other than a Roth IRA) is that the funds are not taxed. You don't have to pay tax on this money until you retire, and you don't have to pay it until you retire with a withdrawal, when you should be in the lower tax bracket of course.

In India, saving for retirement and managing retirement income are two of the most important aspects of financial planning. There are several types of pension plans available to investors. Some of the most common investment options for retirement planning are the Savings Scheme for Seniors (SCSS), National Pension System (NPS), Public Reserve Fund (PPF), bank term deposits, etc. Investors looking to save for retirement may consider opting for safer investment opportunities if they are approaching retirement age.

The risks of investing in a retirement benefit plan are the same as those of buying an investment product in general.

Options (Options):

Options (options) are a more complicated way to buy stocks.

An option (option) is a contract, which is a financial derivative, usually traded based on the value of a stock.

This financial derivative is like a promise and right, you promise and have the right to buy an asset at a certain price for a certain period of time, but you do not necessarily need to act.

For example, let's say you own a car, and you promise your friend that he can buy it for $12,000 within the next month, and you won't sell the car to anyone else during that time. Your friend agrees that he doesn't have to buy the car within the next month, but he has the right to buy the car for $12,000. This commitment is written on the contract,

which is the operating principle of the option (option).
There are two types of options:

- Call Options, which are used to buy an asset; and
- Buy Options, which are used to sell options.

The risk of options is that the value of the asset will decline. If it goes down, you lose money.

Annuities:

Many Americans use annuity insurance as part of a retirement savings plan.

Annuity insurance is where you enter into a contract with an insurance company, and the insurance company pays you regular payments in return.

The insurance company can start paying you money right away, or at a specific date in the future. Annuity insurance can pay until you die or only for an agreed period of time.

Although the risk of annuity insurance is low, the benefits are not high, so it is usually only used as a small part of a retirement savings plan.

Annuities are investments that provide fixed income to investors in India. You can put a lot of money or large corpus in an annuity plan or invest it for a few years and start getting a fixed regular amount out of it.

India offers the following two types of annuity investments:

- immediate annuity
- Deferred annuity

Annuity Immediate is the best investment program or plan in India that allows you to start earning regular income within a month of investing. However, if you want to start earning income within a few years, you can invest in deferred annuity options.

A deferred annuity provides a period of growth for your home or regular investment before generating income.

Cryptocurrencies:

Cryptocurrencies are a relatively recent investment option.

Bitcoin is the most famous cryptocurrency, but there are countless others.

Cryptocurrency is a decentralized digital currency without any government backing. You can trade on cryptocurrency exchanges. Some merchants even let you pay with cryptocurrencies. Cryptocurrencies are usually very volatile, so it is very risky.

Commodities:

Commodities are physical things you can buy.

Commodities may be agricultural products, such as wheat, barley, and corn, or energy products, such as oil, coal, or solar energy.

Precious metals such as gold and silver are the most common commodities.

Usually, investors invest in commodities through futures, or buy physical gold and silver.

The risk of investing in commodities is that the price of the product may fall within a short period of time. For example, politics can have a huge impact on the value of commodities such as oil, while weather can affect the value of agricultural products.

Bank Products:

Banks in India offer reliable investors some of the best investment plans in India. These investments are easy to operate, especially if you have an account with the same bank. Other bank investments include:

- Fixed deposits for pensioners or senior citizens
- fixed deposit
- Gold/Silver Coins and Bars
- Reserve Bank of India Bonds
- Sovereign Gold Bonds
- Portfolio Management Services
- Capital Gains and Deposit Bonds
- non-convertible bonds/debentures
- Tax-Free or tax-exempt bond

While investment banking options in India are full of fixed income and safe investments, they also offer investments in alternative assets. The bank's customized portfolio management services allow you to participate and grow your wealth through a portfolio of equities, debt, real estate and commodities.

In addition to this, you can also invest in commodities such as gold and silver, as well as investment funds. However, these investments require large capital inflows and provide low liquidity. On the other hand, some of the most liquid (i.e. easy to sell) investments in India include working capital and savings accounts.

Real Estate:

Real estate investment is any investment in physical property such as land, buildings, shops, etc. It includes the purchase, ownership and management of real estate. With this type of investment, you can earn a steady income in the form of rent. Another strategy is to buy properties, own them, and then sell them for a higher price at a later point in time to get a decent return on your initial investment. Real estate investment involves the purchase of residential or commercial real estate in order to increase your capital or generate regular rental income.

There are two ways that people can make money from real estate. One way is to buy a property and then sell it for a higher price a few years later. Another way to generate income from your property is to rent it out.

Investors should carefully consider some key factors such as the size and location of the investment property, as these factors play an important role in real-estate appreciation.

Real Estate Investment Tips

If you want a faster appraisal rate, make simple improvements and upgrade your real estate investment. This can significantly increase the market value of your property.

Find out about the additional costs that may arise when buying a property. These can be annual maintenance and upkeep costs, taxes, utility bills, etc.

Owning real estate is one of the basic financial needs of every person. Either way, you will need to invest in at least one residential property in your lifetime. However, real estate in India is also a profitable investment option.

Real estate investment is closely related to national economic development and public policy. Therefore, investing in real estate is also very risky.

Here is how you can invest in different properties:

- buy residential or commercial property
- Buy land for residential or commercial use
- Investing in REITs (Real Estate Investment Trusts)
- Invest in Real Estate Mutual Funds (REMF)

Investing in real estate pays off in two ways:

- fixed rental income
- capital gain

The best part of investing in real estate in India is that the rental income is adjusted for inflation. Thus, investing in real estate to generate rental income is a good option for retirees.

Fixed Deposits:

The most common investment in India is the bank term deposit or fixed deposit (FD).

It offers a fixed interest rate on the principal debt. Almost all term banks in India offer this investment option.

You can open a term deposit account by visiting a bank branch or using Internet banking.

Term deposits or fixed deposits are the most demanded investment direction due to guaranteed fixed income and flexible maturities. Investors make a one-time deposit and earn interest at higher rates than savings accounts. This one-time deposit plus accrued interest is withdrawn at the end of the term. Different banks offer term deposits with different maturities.

In an emergency, an investor can also withdraw their funds early with a small penalty.

The amount of this penalty also varies from bank to bank. A bank term deposit is one of the safest investment options available to investors.

They are offered by banks and other NBFCs and allow investors to deposit free cash at a fixed interest rate for a set period of time. Interest rates are set in advance and do not depend on market fluctuations, which provides a safer investment.

From convenience and flexibility to the variety of options it offers to investors, term deposits are a boon for risk-averse investors. Term deposits offered by banks and non-bank financial institutions are an excellent option for multiplying your funds while maintaining the highest level of security.

Among the different types of investments in India, this option remains popular as it allows you to make a one-time cash deposit with the lender and choose the term that suits your needs. After a predetermined period, your deposit begins to accrue interest at the rate you fixed during the deposit period.

Investment Tips for Fixed Deposits There are penalties for early withdrawals from your FD. Therefore, it is recommended to choose a suitable deposit period after carefully evaluating your future financial goals.

While FDs are generally considered a risk-free type of investment in some cases, they also come with some risk. If the bank fails, you will be insured for 5 lakhs per depositor in the bank. By spreading your investments across different banks, you can effectively protect the majority of your finances.

Public Provident Fund (PPF):

Provident funds constitute a significant part of your retirement corpus. Provident fund is a mandatory, government-sponsored retirement scheme that aims at providing employees with a lump sum payment when the employee resigns or during retirement. Public Provident Fund is another fixed income savings scheme started by the Government of India. Under this scheme, the interest on your principal investment is paid by the government.

Investment up to ?1,50,000 is tax-deductible and interest earned on this amount is also tax-free. Considered to be one of the safest options among the different types of investment in India, Public Provident Fund is an instrument backed by the government. While opening the account, the minimum investment amount is as low as Rs.100 in some of the banks.

Thereafter, the annual limits for PPF deposits range from a minimum of Rs.500 to a maximum of Rs.1.5 lakh. These investment types come with a lock-in period of 15 years and are eligible for tax deductions under section 80C of the Income Tax Act, 1961.

Investment Tips for PPF

PPF is the best investment option in India to build a tax-free corpus of funds, as the maturity amount from this saving scheme is completely exempt from tax. The minimum investment tenure for the plan is 15 years. You can extend the account after maturity in batches of 5-years.

You can withdraw money partially after five financial years of investment.

Before partial withdrawals, you can borrow from the accumulated corpus if need be.

National Pension System (NPS):

The National Pension System Trust is a specialized division of the Pension Fund Regulatory and Development Authority under the jurisdiction of the Ministry of Finance, Government of India. The National Pension Scheme is a voluntary defined contribution pension scheme in India.

NPS is a savings scheme administered and regulated by the Pension Fund Regulatory Authority of India. It collects money from many investors and then invests the corpus in various equity and debt securities.

This savings scheme is primarily intended for building a pension corpus. Regular investments throughout your working life are partially withdrawn at retirement, and the remaining amount is paid out as a regular pension.

Any Indian citizen between the ages of 18-60 can open an NPS account. The maturity of the account occurs at the age of 60 with the possibility of extension up to 70 years. Partial withdrawals of up to 25% are allowed after 3 years of account opening.

The National Pension Scheme is another investment scheme supported by the Government of India. It falls under the types of investments in India that focus on long-term savings, making it a perfect addition to your retirement investment plan.

You can choose from two different types of investment options, i.e. active withdrawal or automatic withdrawal. With an automatic selection investment, the ratio of investments in different asset classes is predetermined. In the active option, you can determine the asset allocation according to your preferences. If you are financially savvy, you can choose an active selection of investment options.

Unit Linked Insurance Plan (ULIP):

Unit Linked Insurance Plans are among the types of investments that come with tax benefits in India.

It is a tool that offers you an investment advantage along with insurance. The premium you pay to stay in the investment is divided into two parts.

One part is aimed at providing you with a protective life insurance policy, while the other invests in market-linked instruments or funds.

ULIPs also provide deductions under the Income Tax Act 1961 under applicable tax laws because the premium paid is deductible and the term benefits and long-term capital gains tax-free. Unit Linked Insurance Plans or ULIPs are unique life insurance plus investment plans.

Each ULIP offers multiple funds as investment options.

At the same time, ULIPs also offer life insurance for the policyholder. Life insurance ensures that your family reaches the goal even after your untimely death. Also, ULIP plans offer automated portfolio management options for aggressive investors.

These options allow you to automatically manage your investment risk based on market movement or investment timing.

Investment Tips for ULIPs

Note the fees you may incur when investing in this type of investment. These may include premium allocation fees, administrative fees, fund management fees, death fees, and more. Invest in ULIP from a minimum fee insurance provider.

- Choose a ULIP that provides the optimum amount of flexibility.
- You should choose customizable plans with different funding options that offer flexibility in terms of premium payments.
- To meet the needs of different types of investors in India, ULIPs allow you to easily direct your premiums and change funds according to market movements and evolving risk appetite.

ULIPs are types of investments that offer the flexibility to choose an asset allocation strategy based on risk appetite and goal in mind.

Senior Citizens' Savings Scheme:

Indian residents over the age of 60 can open an SCSS account and invest in this scheme for a block of 5 years. 15 lakhs to your SCSS account in multiples of Rs. 1 lakh can be done in cash. 1 lakh is to be made using sight draft or check.

Investments in SCSS are also eligible for deduction under Section 80C, up to a limit of Rs. 1.5 million.

CHAPTER THIRTEEN

ADVICE FOR BEGINNERS

Balance your online portfolio

To help you avoid investment risk, you can balance your portfolio by diversifying your investments across different asset classes. Some of the different asset classes include:

- stock or share capital
- Bonds and Fixed Income Securities
- Cash Equivalents and Money Market

The importance of a personal investment plan

A personal investment plan can help you sort out your finances and understand how long it will take to reach your goals. You can create a plan and adjust it over time as your lifestyle and circumstances change.

What kind of investments are suitable for new investors? Advice for beginners

Figuring out where to invest can be a big challenge for beginners in investing.

In this age of the Internet, we can find a lot of investment information. But sometimes too much information can make people lose their way.

What types of investments are suitable for beginners?

When you're just starting out with investing, you want to start with the most basic, most sound. These types of investments include:

1. The stock market

Stocks are the most common and easiest to understand type of investment.

When you buy stock in a company, you own a small part of the company.

When companies are profitable, they pay you a portion of the profits, which we call dividends (or dividends).

As the value of the company goes up, so does the price of your stock, which means you can sell your stock for a profit in the future.

2. Invest in bonds:

Bonds are loans. When you buy a company or government bond, you are lending your money to the company or government.

Companies or governments often raise money by selling bonds, and they pay you interest for the time you lend the company or government money. Just like when you borrow money from the bank, the bank will charge you interest.

Investing in bonds generally has lower risk and lower returns than stocks.

3. Mutual Funds:

A mutual fund is a portfolio of stocks of multiple companies. When you buy a fund, you buy shares of multiple companies at the same time.

Mutual funds are usually classified by investment in different industries or fields. For example, emerging market funds mainly invest in emerging markets, and Southeast Asia real estate funds mainly invest in real estate in Southeast Asia.

There are also several different types of investments in mutual funds, the most popular being index funds and ETFs.

An index fund is a fund based on the performance of a specific index (such as the commonly-heard S&P 500, nifty, Sensex, etc.). If the Index rises, the index fund will follow.

An ETF exchange-traded fund is to sell the fund in the form of stocks. For example, you can buy an ETF to make it easier for investors to trade the fund.

Generally, mutual funds are managed by a fund manager, who is responsible for researching the market, selecting stocks and tracking the performance of the fund, so investors need to pay management fees.

This is why index funds and ETFs are very popular, because index funds do not require the management of fund managers, and the fees are relatively low, while ETFs are traded in the form of stocks, and one share may be very cheap, which is relatively cost-effective for investment funds.

4. Physical goods:

You can invest in physical commodities like precious metals gold and silver.

Gold and silver are usually the best insurance in times of economic downturn. Gold and silver have an important place in our monetary history, they have a certain store of value and are often used to overcome inflation.

5. Savings Account:

This is the least risky way to invest. Put your money in a savings account that generates interest.

Unfortunately, many banks now offer interest rates that cannot keep up with inflation. This means that interest on savings accounts cannot keep up with rising prices.

So if you want to invest through a savings account, you need to find a savings account with high enough interest to really pay off.

Remember, when choosing an investment product at the beginning, the most important thing is to choose a product that can "generate additional income in the long term" for you.

For example, "value investing" in the stock market is a method that many people have proven successful and rich, and it is also more suitable for beginners.

If you are interested in short-term investing, you can also make money by buying and selling stocks.

However, this also means that you need to do a lot of homework first, otherwise it will become a "luck" transaction, and it is easy to put the cart before the horse and lose money instead of making money.

Whichever method you choose, investing should help you generate additional income. Many people often forget this after investing.

Which entry-level investment types offer good returns?

Often small returns are easy, and the risk is low. For example, you can buy Treasury bonds, and you can almost guarantee a 2-3% annual return.

If 2-3% fails to meet your investment goals, you can choose to invest in stocks.

If you think you don't understand much about the world's big companies, you've always heard of iPhone, Jobs, Google, Microsoft, Bill Gates, Tesla, Amazon, Wipro, Tata, Reliance, Infosys, Sbi, Hdfc, Icici, etc ... These companies are growing and developing strongly, no matter what challenges the market faces. Such challenges, they should be able to survive. So as a beginner in investing, you can start by becoming a minority shareholder in these companies.

Besides stocks, you can also consider investing in indices.

Over the past 10 years, the average annual return for the S&P 500, nifty, Sensex has been equal or greater than 9.8%.

This means that if you invest your money in the index fund, you don't have to spend time researching stocks, and you can still expect to earn 3-4 times more than investing in bonds, and more than 10 times more than savings accounts.

How to start investing in funds? Getting Started with Investment Funds.

Funds are a very convenient and easy way to invest for beginners.

How to start an investment fund? You can start learning how to invest in funds by following these 5 steps:

- Decide whether you prefer active or passive funds
- Calculate budgets and save costs
- Fund selection should be diversified
- Deciding where to buy the fund
- Build and manage your portfolio and stick to it

Decide whether you prefer active or passive funds

The first big decision you'll have to make is whether you want to buy an active fund or a lower-cost passive fund.

Active funds are actively managed by professionals. These fund managers hope to outperform passive funds and the general market by actively managing funds. Active funds usually require higher costs because of the need for human intervention in management.

While active funds sound like they have more potential than passive funds, it turns out that while many fund managers outperform in the short term, few active funds outperform passive funds in the long term. So, unless you have a lot of confidence in a fund manager, choosing a passive foundation is a more cost-effective option.

Passive funds are generally cheaper and require no human management. For investors, passive funds are quite convenient and can bring good returns.

One of the benchmark passive funds is the index fund. An index fund invests in multiple securities, and its performance is representative of the performance of the entire market. For example, the shares held by an S&P 500 index fund are modelled after the well-known 500 stock index, and the S&P 500 index fund itself performs the same as the S&P 500 index. This means that if the news says the S&P 500 is up 3%, it means your index fund is up 3%.

Because passive funds don't require much management, their fees are lower than active funds.

Calculate your budget and save costs

No matter which type of fund you choose, you need to consider your investment budget and how you can save money. When it comes to budgeting, ideally you can make long-term investments that don't need to be moved for at least 5 years.

Usually, fund providers have minimum capital requirements for investment and account opening. Some brokerages have no minimum capital requirements; others may have minimum capital requirements.

The benefit of funds is that you don't need a lot of capital to have a diversified portfolio (both stocks and bonds).

As for the cost of investment, the first and most important thing is - try not to pay the advance payment when you buy the fund, because it means that you have already paid a part of the fee to the broker before you buy the fund, and you are not sure about this The foundation does not increase your funds.

Another important point is to pay attention to the management fees of the fund. If an active fund's annual fee of more than 1% is probably too high, its performance after costs may not be as good as the market generally does. Passive funds have fees below 0.1%, so if you choose to invest in index funds, you'll pay very little in terms of fees.

Fund selection should be diversified

When buying a fund, you should pay attention to whether your fund invests in different fields. If you buy all 5 funds that track the S&P 500, then it's no different than buying just 1 S&P 500 fund.

Diversification is important, and having a well-balanced set of funds is more beneficial than having multiple funds. You should try investing in funds in different sectors, such as different industries, stocks, bonds, real estate or other alternative investments. In different areas, you can try to find other ways to diversify your portfolio, such as funds of overseas stocks and funds of US stocks.

This way, your portfolio will be more balanced and able to perform well in different market conditions.

Decide where to buy the fund

There are 3 ways to buy funds:

- Buy directly from the fund company
- Buy from an investment firm that manages a portfolio of funds
- Buy through a broker

The cheapest way is to go directly to a fund company to buy their funds, or open an account with a portfolio investment company that offers stocks and manages funds.

The disadvantage of buying funds directly from a fund company is that you can only buy funds from their company, there is no other option. The same is true for managed fund portfolio investment companies, except for their own managed fund portfolios, you will not find other options within the company, and the degree of freedom is relatively low.

However, if a managed fund portfolio investment company provides a portfolio of funds you like, you only need to make a single deposit to invest in multiple funds you want to invest in, and the managed fund portfolio investment company will regularly issue dividends to you.

If you prefer to choose your own funds, you can choose to buy funds through a brokerage. In this way, you can access a variety of funds in various fields without limitation.

Build and manage your portfolio and stick to it

After buying the fund, remember not to be too slack. Your job doesn't end there, you also need to track your funds regularly to make sure your investments are ok.

If you choose an active fund, remember to track whether the fund's performance is as good as the fund company says after a period of time, and if they change the fund manager, does the new manager perform the same as the old one, or does it actually make a difference?

If you choose to invest in an index fund, a change in the benchmark index may indicate a change in the fund's performance, so it's up to you to decide whether this is consistent with your investment objectives and strategy.

On top of that, if the fund's expense ratio increases, it may not bode well.

The funds themselves are long-term and diversified portfolios, so you don't need to feel too stressed and tracked 24 hours a day. But it's good for you to schedule time to track and review your fund investments on a regular basis.

CHAPTER FOURTEEN

Fundamental Principles of Financial Management

Organize your finances

Organizing your finances is the first step in creating wealth. Credit cards, bank accounts, personal loans, brokerage accounts, mortgages, auto loans, and retirement accounts should all be tracked. Budgeting software can provide a complete solution to keep track of all these accounts, pay on time, and more.

Spend less than you earn

Personal finance software provides powerful tools to help you track and budget your spending and take steps to achieve your long-term goals. If you learn to keep track of your finances and know where you spend the most money, you can control your money. "The best way to make sure you get over debt or avoid it in the first place is to never spend more than you earn," Morris said.

Put your money to work

Use the time value of money. Morris gives the following example. "A 21-year-old who invests $17.50 a day until retirement at age 65, with an average annual investment return of 5%, can become a millionaire. At age 30, the required daily savings amount nearly doubles. At 40, that amount quadruples." So save early and often, even small amounts.

Limit debt to income-generating assets

With credit cards and auto loans, every penny you spend paying off your debt is money going down the drain. With the exception of a few models with zero depreciation, more repairs and finance costs are required than can reasonably be expected to be returned to the owner when sold. Morris explained: "With its sky-high interest rates, a credit card for buying household items and clothes that wear out quickly is not a good idea. If you must go into debt, stick to funding projects that will hold their value long-term. Like real estate and education."

Keep educating yourself

Budgeting software is often linked to a wealth of research, putting the collective knowledge of Wall Street at your fingertips. " Read every financial journal, book, and blog you can find, written by respected financial authors." " Understand why you're investing, so you'll stick with your plan. Gather research regularly, so you don't miss out on great investment opportunities."

Understand risk

The key to understanding the return on investment is that the greater your risk, the better the return should be. This is called the risk-reward trade-off. Investments with higher returns, like stocks and bonds, tend to carry a higher risk of losing the principal you invested. Investments with lower returns, such as certificates of deposit and money market accounts, carry a lower risk of losing their principal. Since no one knows the future, you cannot be 100% sure that any investment will turn out well. "If you diversify your investments, one investment can go bad without seriously affecting your overall portfolio,".

Diversification is not just for investing

Find creative ways to diversify your income. Everyone has their own talents or special skills. " Turn your talent into an opportunity to earn money. Investigate ways to make money from home and start a home-based business," Morris said. The extra income can supplement your full-time income and even lead to an exciting career change. Good financial management software can tell you that even a small increase in income can positively change your financial situation.

Make the most of your employment benefits

Employment benefits like 401(k) plans, flexible spending accounts, and medical and dental insurance can yield some of the highest rates of return you can get. " Make sure you're taking advantage of all the benefits that can save you money by reducing taxes or out-of-pocket payments,".

Pay attention to taxes

Financial planning software can help you manage your tax information. For example, Quicken can quickly analyze taxable investments and provide powerful tools to make year-end tax filing smoother. " We all know that any money you make is taxed," Morris stressed. "That's why it's important to consider the tax implications of each investment."

Plan for the unexpected

Despite your best efforts, you will face unforeseen emergencies. " Save enough money and stock up on insurance to be able to deal with long-term unemployment, accidents, catastrophic medical care, major auto or home repairs and natural disasters,". Increasing your savings during good times can help you manage the cost impact of bumps and make sure unexpected financial risks don't derail your long-term goals and your family's financial security.

CHAPTER FIFTEEN

How to analyse stocks? Understand basic stock analysis methods at a time

When investing in stocks, your goal is to find stocks that are "priced below the future value of the company."

It is not easy to accurately predict the future profits of a company and whether it will grow. After all, no one can predict the future. But we can use stock analysis to help us invest.

Stock analysis can help you find the best investment opportunities. Through a variety of analytical methods, we can try to find stocks that are trading below their intrinsic value to capture future gains.

How to do stock analysis? Teaching stock analysis beginners

View the company's business introduction

The first step is to understand the main business of the company to be analyzed and its industry classification, to have a general understanding of the business scope and revenue sources of the analyzed company. If you find that you still can't clearly understand what the company's business is, before proceeding to the next step, investors need to study it more deeply. If you can't understand it because it involves too much professional knowledge, please give up the investment.

Industry prospect analysis

After understanding the company's business, this step requires investors to use the tentacles of the surrounding political, economic and social environment to assess whether the company's industry prospects are ideal. If the industry is on an upward trajectory, then it is beneficial to invest in the company; but if it is judged to be a sunset industry, it does not mean that all companies in the industry should not invest, but to analyze whether the company has the planning and ability to transform.

Read and review

Read and review the company's most recent annual chairman's report and management discussion and analysis

The third step is to download the company's most recent interim or unscheduled annual report. The chairman's report, management discussion and analysis are usually located at the beginning of the annual report. By reading this content, you can intuitively know the company's performance in the past year. Outlook for the future, which business is growing or shrinking, industry trends, and the advantages and difficulties of the company's operations. Through such content, investors can grasp the general situation of the company, which is helpful for making trading decisions. Investors can also judge the company's ability to meet expectations when the next quarterly report is published to analyze the company's management's ability to execute.

Watch the Investor Presentation

Many investors ignore the company's performance presentation. Usually, the company's performance presentation is held on the same day as the annual report. The company's management reports the company's performance and outlook. More importantly, investors can get the response in the Q&A session in the annual report. Information that cannot be known, such as the more specific direction of capital use, the rise and fall of expected net interest rates, and other issues that investors value.

However, not all companies conduct performance presentations. However, this also reflects that companies with performance presentations focus more on their relationship with investors, which also strengthens investors' confidence in the company.

Read the company's most recent financial statements

Before analyzing financial statements, investors must have a basic knowledge of the income statement and balance sheet, such as understanding the concepts of fixed/variable costs, depreciation and goodwill. The most important thing in analyzing financial statements is to calculate the different financial indicators of the company, including return on equity (ROE), profit margin (Profit Margin), current/quick ratio (Current/Quick ratio), etc. Comparison to analyze whether the company's financial position and cash flow have improved and grown. The above is only a small part of the analysis of financial statements, and it will not be described in detail due to the limited space. It is worth mentioning that investors should pay more attention to the notes to the financial statements in the company's annual report, which may hide unexpected details.

Peer analysis

After having a general understanding of the company's operation and financial status, investors should study its competition in the same industry and potential competitors to analyze whether the company has a comparative advantage and calculate whether its future potential profits will be reduced due to competitors. Investors can directly compare financial ratios such as return on equity, profit margins and debt levels among peer companies, or they can use different analytical models proposed by Michael Porter, the father of competitive strategy, such as Competitor Analysis.) or market segmentation analysis (Segmentation Analysis) and other frameworks for peer analysis.

Calculate the intrinsic value of the company

This step is very important, but it is also a step that many small investors ignore (or have no concept of at all). Investors should attempt to calculate the intrinsic value of the company based on the information obtained above. There are also various methods for calculating value, including absolute valuation methods such as discounted cash flow method (Discounted Cash Flow), option pricing method (Black-Scholes); there are also relative valuation methods such as enterprise value multiple {EV/EBITDA} and price-to-book ratio (PB) valuation methods. The valuation methods applied to vary from company to company. Investors can also read the research reports and target prices provided by the research sections of different financial institutions as reference for valuation.

Waiting for the time to buy

After investors have calculated the intrinsic value of the company in their minds, they can wait for the company's share price to fall to a desired level of safety margin. When the stock price falls to the ideal purchase level in the future, it is also necessary to pay attention to whether the reason for the decline is caused by changes in the stock fundamentals, otherwise investors should re-value the company.

If you are confident that the stock price is too high above its intrinsic value, you can also buy a put option or go short.

CHAPTER SIXTEEN

Fundamental Analysis and Technical Analysis

There are two basic ways to analyse stocks:

fundamental analysis and technical analysis.

Fundamental analysis:

Fundamental analysis is based on the assumption that stock prices do not necessarily reflect the true intrinsic value of a company. Fundamental analysts use value measures and other information about a company's business to determine whether a stock's price is attractive. If your investment goals are long-term, fundamental analysis is your best bet.

Technical analysis:

Technical analysis is based on the assumption that "stock prices will change based on available information and trends". In other words, technical analysts believe that you can predict future price action based on historical fluctuations in stock prices. If you see people trying to find patterns in stock charts, or talking about moving averages, that's a type of technical analysis. Technical analysis is usually used for short-term trading, and the risk of trading is relatively high.

Basically, fundamental analysis is used to find long-term investment opportunities while technical analysis is used to profit from short-term price fluctuations.

The most effective way is to start with direct practice

Just like learning to ride a bicycle or learning a new language, direct practice reading analyst reports is the most effective way to help you start analyzing stocks yourself, and it will save you a lot of time.

In the beginning, your goal is not to blindly follow the recommendations made by analysts, but to try to quickly understand the situation of the company from reading their research reports, including the company's strengths and weaknesses, major competitors, industry prospects and future prospects.

There is a lot of information in analyst research reports, and reading research reports from different analysts will also help you identify commonalities. Opinions may vary from analyst to analyst, but the underlying facts are the same in all reports.

Additionally, you can pay special attention to earnings forecasts from different analysts, who may have different price targets for the same stock. When reading the report, also remember to find out the reasons behind the analyst's vacated conclusions.

Several well-known analyst reports on the Internet include Zacks Investment Research , Morningstar, Seeking Alpha, screener, finology, etc., many of which can be registered for free to obtain reports.

6 metrics commonly used in stock analysis

There are 6 of the most important and easy-to-understand metrics in the analytics tool that you'll often see in analyst reports. These metrics are:

- Earnings per share (EPS)
- Price to earnings ratio (P/E ratio)
- Price-to-earnings growth ratio (PEG ratio)
- Price-to-book ratio (P/B ratio)
- Return on Equity (ROE)
- Debt to EBITDA ratio (Debt/EBITDA ratio)

Earnings Per Share (EPS)

Public companies report earnings per share (EPS) to shareholders, and if the company earns $1 million in a period and the company has 1 million shares, then the company's earnings per share are $1 per share.

1,000,000 (earnings) ÷ 1,000,000 (number of shares) = 1 (earnings per share)

So an increase in EPS is a good sign for investors. According to the Nasdaq, the higher a company's earnings per share, the more valuable your stock is. The higher the earnings, the more investors want to buy the company's stock.

A small reminder: EPS and dividends both reflect a company's earnings, but are used for different purposes. Earnings per share is a measure of a company's stock's ability to make profits, while dividends are a calculation of what percentage of a company's earnings are received by shareholders.

Price to earnings ratio (P/E ratio)

The price-to-earnings ratio (P/E ratio) is a company's current share price divided by its earnings per share, usually measured in one year. If the stock is trading at $30, and the company's earnings over the past year are $2 per share, we'd say the company's stock has a price-to-earnings ratio of 15.

30 (current share price) ÷ 2 (earnings per share) = 15 (price-earnings ratio)

The higher the price-earnings ratio, the higher the stock price and the lower the earnings per share, which also means that the stock price may be too high. The price-to-earnings ratio is the most common measure of value in fundamental analysis, and is most useful when comparing companies in the same industry and with similar prospects.

Price-to-earnings growth ratio (PEG ratio)

The price-earnings ratio (PEG ratio) is an extension of the price-earnings ratio (P/E ratio). Different companies grow at different rates, so it's important to factor this into stock research as well.

Price-to-earnings growth divides the price-to-earnings ratio by the expected annual earnings growth over the next few years. If the company's stock price-earnings ratio is 20, and you expect the company's earnings to be 10% over the next 5 years, then the stock's P/E growth rate over the next 5 years is 2.

20(P/E ratio) ÷ 10(Expected earnings rate) = 2(P/E growth rate)

The higher the price-earnings growth rate, the higher the price-earnings ratio and the slower the expected earnings rate, which also means that the stock price may be too high relative to the company's growth rate. The price-earnings growth rate allows you to compare the stock prices of companies that are growing faster and slower over the same time period.

Price-to-book ratio (P/B ratio)

Price-to-book ratio (P/B ratio) A comparison of a company's stock price and its book value.

A company's book value is the sum of its assets. Book value is an accounting term, and you can imagine it as if you sold all the company's assets - both tangible and intangible assets, such as machines, office chairs, patents, brands, etc. - the company What is the value of .

The price-to-book ratio is calculated by dividing the company's stock price by the book value per share. If a company's book value is $1 million, the company has 100,000 shares, and the stock price is $20 per share, then the company's book value per share is $10 per share, and the company's price-to-book ratio is 2.

1,000,000(book value) ÷ 100,000(number of shares) = 10(book value per share)

20(stock price) ÷ 10(book value per share) = 2(book value per share)

The higher the price-to-book ratio, the higher the stock price, and the lower the book value per share, which means the stock price may be too high. Price-to-book ratios are best for increasingly comparing companies in the same industry with similar growth characteristics.

Return on equity (ROE)

Return on Equity (ROE) is most often used as a measure of a company's profitability.

Assuming that both Company A and Company B have earnings of $500,000 this year, Company A has $1 million in assets invested by shareholders, and Company B has $2 million, the return on equity for both companies is calculated as

Company A: 500,000 (earnings) ÷ 1,000,000 (shareholders' assets) = 0.5 = 50% (return on equity)

Company B: 500,000 (earnings) ÷ 2,000,000 (shareholders' assets) = 0.25 = 25% (return on equity)

Company B has more assets, but the income it generates is the same as that of Company A, which means that Company A is more efficient than Company B in generating income, which means that the higher the return on equity, the more profitable the company is. The higher the ability.

Debt to EBITDA ratio, Debt/EBITDA ratio

EBITDA is the abbreviation of earnings before interest, taxes, depreciation, and amortization, Chinese is the income before interest, taxes, depreciation and amortization.

A company's financial health should also be taken into account when analysing a company's stock, and one good way to look at the company's debt profile is to use the debt-to-EBITDA ratio.

On the company's balance sheet you can find the company's total liabilities and on the income statement you can find EBITDA. Divide total debt by EBITDA to get your ratio.

The higher the ratio, the higher the investment risk.

Basic Stock Analysis Case

Let's take the past 12 months of data from Southwest Airlines (NYSE:LUV) and Delta Air Lines (NYSE:DAL) as an example:

Metrics. Southwest Airlines (LUV). Delta Air Lines (DAL)

Earnings per share (EPS) $3.4 $5.39

P/E ratio 8.01 4.2

PEG ratio 0.68 0.22

P/B ratio 1.55 1.01

Return on Equity (ROE) 18.73% 24.45%

Debt to EBITDA ratio 1.75 4.65

Data source: gurufocus, 2020/5/9

In terms of earnings per share, Delta is doing better than Southwest.

In terms of P/E, Delta is cheaper, but if we factor in P/E growth, Southwest is a bit higher than Delta.

If we look at ROE, we will find that Delta is more efficient than Southwest, but Delta also has higher debt, which means higher investment risk.

Use data to help you find good stocks

There is no one-size-fits-all way to assess a stock's value, but the basic metrics mentioned above should give you a quick idea of how a company is doing. Many analysts' reports also include these metrics, so knowing what's behind them can help you understand what's in them more easily when you read the report.

If you're not sure where to find this data, enter the information you're looking for into a search engine. Many companies provide this data for free; you don't need to calculate each one, the most important thing is to know how to interpret and compare the data.

CHAPTER SEVENTEEN

HOW TO MANAGE THE MONEY YOU EARN?

When it comes to saving money and managing money, I personally think that they are two completely non-conflicting concepts. Saving money is the original accumulation of capital, while financial investment is the more effective use of accumulated capital to achieve more capital accumulation. From this perspective, saving money and managing wealth is a small cycle of capital accumulation, and it can be carried out at the same time.

Needless to say, saving money is a way of capital accumulation. It is the inheritance of the traditional Chinese virtue of diligence and thrift. As long as there is a planned and reasonable consumption, this is not a job that requires much brainpower.

Financial management is completely different. There are certain risks in personal investment and financial management. Therefore, you must be cautious. You must understand and master some basic knowledge and skills of financial management. The two most basic principles are that investors, especially beginners, must know of??

Don't follow what others say, stick to rational financial management??

The mentality of "conforming to the crowd" is also ubiquitous in investment and financial management. Many people do not have their own judgement and planning when investing. They just look at where everyone invests and get together. They feel that it is the same as shopping in a supermarket. Everyone is rushing to buy. Good thing, this is extremely undesirable.

Everyone should formulate their own investment and financial planning according to their own situation, choose suitable financial products, learn more about investment and financial management, and enrich themselves, so that they can go longer.

The way to live with more money has more money, and the way to live with less money has less money.

The premise is to know the composition of family members, so that we can analyze in detail. The situation of children and the elderly, etc.,

In terms of money, it's still the same sentence. You have to increase your income and reduce expenditure. Find a way to make more money, and reduce your expenses as much as you can. Of course, you can't reduce the cost of eating. People who work so hard to earn money are not for eating better and making money. Don't bring what you don't bring. The most important thing is to earn more. Even if you two don't eat or drink, it will only cost you tens of thousands of dollars a year.

So, you have to find a way to earn more, especially when you are young. When you are strong. When you get older, you can't keep up with your mental and physical strength. Your whole life will pass like this, and the decades of rushing and rushing will be over. No matter how hard you work, whether you have money or no money, anyway, it's all a way of passing, this is one's own choice.

WARREN BUFFETT'S 3 FAMOUS QUOTES CAN HELP YOU STABILISE YOUR EMOTIONS IN A BEAR MARKET

In the face of the repeated market conditions of the global stock market in recent months, if you want to ride out the bear market safely, the following are three investment principles of Warren Buffett, which are worth revisiting again and again.

1. Greed when markets panic

Buffett's most important quote: **"We are fearful when others are greedy, and greedy only when others are fearful."**

You'll never really know how hard it is until the market gets scary, but this quote is an incredible reminder that in the short term, markets are driven by emotion. When the mood turns sour, level-headed investors often encounter incredible opportunities.

Falling stocks in a portfolio are often easy to focus on, but if it's real value, it's more of a buying opportunity than nothing to worry about. In addition, you don't need to try to get the lowest price, you just need to increase your holdings if you have idle funds when you are in a relative panic.

2. Don't lose money

Another of Buffett's most widely quoted: **"The first rule of investing is not to lose money, and the second rule of investing is not to forget the first."**

On the surface, this seems simple and completely lacking in useful information. But to grasp this principle, you must understand how investors lose money in the stock market. The only way to actually lose money is to sell stocks when there is a loss. This leads to an important distinction: A falling stock price doesn't indicate a sell. The only reason to sell a stock at a loss is if the underlying investment thesis that originally bought it is no longer true.

Buffett believes that when you buy a stock, you have to be prepared for a drop of 50% or more and still be comfortable with it. In fact, Berkshire's stock has fallen by 50%. So if the only rule in investing is to avoid losses, you should avoid selling battered stocks unless the underlying business is fundamentally flawed.

3. Don't check prices every day

Buffett once said, **"If you've made good investments in securities, you shouldn't be bothered even if you close the stock market for five years."**

As an investor, you need to understand the importance of taking a long-term hold. However, for different reasons, or just curiosity, we look at stock prices every day. The two are reversed. If the stock market were to close for 5 years, would you be satisfied or worried about the holdings in your portfolio? If you're confident, a bear market shouldn't scare you. It's easier said than done, of course, but avoiding daily stock checks can take the pressure off market volatility.

About The Author

Prem Amrit is an investor, entrepreneur, digital marketing and social media expert, graphic designer,web developer and writer, consultant, writer based in Bihar.He is the author of the book Financial Intelligence.

In 2006, he worked as a visual effects artist and digital artist on many Bollywood and Hollywood films. After working for over ten years, He has started investing in the Indian stock market in 2020, and he has a successful history of finding some multibagger stocks As now, in 2022, he will try his luck in writing. prem enjoys playing carom, painting, photography, reading books and travelling.

www.ingramcontent.com/pod-product-compliance
Lightning Source LLC
Chambersburg PA
CBHW022015150726
47990CB00002B/661